CLIMB EVERY OBSTACLE
Eliminate Your Limits!

Anita Jefferson

"Courage and perseverance have a magical talisman
before which difficulties disappear and obstacles
vanish into air."
John Quincy Adams

Climb Every Obstacle:: Eliminate Your Limits

Printed in the United States by
RealWord Publications
Norcross, GA
Copyright 2004

PO Box 931461
Norcross, GA 30093-1461

ISBN:
0-9743088-0-3

Cover design: Sandy Belk, Belk Publications

Dedications

This book is dedicated to those who know my fights
and have stood in the ring of life with me:
my parents, Frank and Gracie Jefferson,
Roderick and Joyce Jefferson,
Alger Jefferson (my twin),
Frank Jefferson, III
Mary Wooten Lacey
Brett and Karen Blake
Elizabeth O. Johnson
and to Gary who taught me:
"I am the child of a rich Father.
I deserve the best, for it is MY right."

About the Author

It took Anita many years of contemplation, therapy, regression, and success to climb her obstacles. After two strokes, a near fatal car accident, recovery from numerous surgeries, and the survival of two cases of near fatal pulmonary emboli, she had much from and for which to climb. In spite of all of the sobering medical and physical predictions, she did climb and continues to climb, obstacle by obstacle she ascends.

She was taught how to love and to give by her parents. As she matured into an adult, she learned many other lessons, many of which you'll find herein. Also, she learned of her powerlessness and God's might. She has learned the meaning of service. Most importantly, she learned not to fear.

Climb Every Obstacle forces the definite.

Photo by Thad Taylor

The Road Not Taken

Two roads diverged in a yellow wood,
And sorry I could not travel both
And be one traveler, long I stood
And looked down one as far as I could
To where it bent in the undergrowth;

Then took the other, as just as fair,
And having perhaps the better claim,
Because it was grassy and wanted wear
Though as for that the passing there
Had worn them really about the same,

And both that morning equally lay
In leaves no step had trodden black.
Oh, I kept the first for another day!
Yet knowing how way leads onto way,
I doubted if I should ever come back.

I shall be telling this with a sigh
Somewhere ages and ages hence;
Two roads diverged in a wood, and I-
I took the one less traveled by,
And that has made all the difference.
—Robert Frost (1916)

In Tribute

One of my favorite sayings is:
"When life gives you lemons, make lemonade."
Lemonade is my drink of choice.

Dr. Jennifer Kelly
Dawn-Breakers Toastmasters Club
National Speakers Association Georgia
Nasif and Vernada Habaeeb'u'llah
The Ataie Family
Jamila Canady
Lynda Shorter
Alfred and Michelle Wiseman
Sandy Belk
Antionette Bianchi

You have been the sweetener in my lemonade mix.
Thank you for being so sweet to me.

My Happiness Lemonade recipe:
1 gallon of joy juice
2 quarts of service
3 liters of smile elixir
4 teardrops
5 tablespoons of exercise
6 ounces of affirmations
7 grams of yellow daises
8 pints of serenity
9 servings of prayer

Contents

Preface

Climb Every Obstacle is arranged so you can read an obstacle a day or select your most challenging obstacles for your inspiration. It is written in a clear, straightforward, and encouraging tone to promote a consciousness of vitality and success.

The right hand page is a passageway. It may have an inspiring story about someone who has overcome that particular fear-evoking obstacle or the page may contain a quote, a poem, a proverb or scripture reading for you to affirm your inner strength. The left hand page is about the obstacle. It opens with a quote and is a direct message to you. At the end of the page is an opportunity step that requires you to take action. Within two pages you can examine the obstacle, focus on possibilities for you, and then exercise the opportunity step.

Obstacles are a part of everyone's life DNA. You are not alone in this trek to overcoming them in order to magnify your potential. Read Climb Every Obstacle obstacle by obstacle. It may be more effective for you to select the obstacles that are more prominent for you now or you may choose to read the book in alphabetical order. Whichever method you decide to use, take time to ponder the thoughts, maxims, and quotes carefully selected therein. Ingest the inspiration. Inculcate the message to believe in yourself. Embrace your gifts without fear so that you can advance the world. Lastly, celebrate the steps you take each day as part of your upward climb to your Great Destiny.

Be better tomorrow because of yesterday.

Our destiny changes with our thought. We shall become what we wish to become; do what we wish to do; when our habitual thought corresponds with our desire.

Orson S. Marden
Founder, Success magazine

Climb Every Obstacle:: Eliminate Your Limits

Fear is the dark unknown
A feeling your way with guideposts unseen;
A cautious planting of one foot before the other.
A crouched position as if your head cannot lead.
There is nothing certain about fear except that it comes.

Our action becomes the unknown.
Fear injects us with a growth opportunity
It rings internal warnings like flags raising,
It signals the brain for physical and mental energy.
There is nothing certain about fear except action®.

—Barbara Collier

FEAR

"Fear is that little darkroom where negatives are developed."
—Michael Prithard

FEAR is the element common of every obstacle in this book. It is the trademark of the ego. Uncontrolled fear precipitates many types of dysfunction and when taken to the extreme, fear is the basis of dysthymia, severe depression or suicide.

Fear is relative. There are two types of fear: real or imagined. Real fear is a response to eminent or potential danger. The senses are alert, heightened to danger so that the body can quickly react.

Imagined fear arises from projected expectancies or exaggerated concerns. In anticipation of what may happen, the body and mind is over stimulated needlessly. Staying in a constant state of alert overworks the endocrine system and is the cause of chronic anxiety. The emotional outcome of which is panic attacks.

Though vastly different in origin, whether real or imagined fear, the body response is the same—you experience a rush of excitement caused by the secretion of adrenaline. Fear can morph into many forms. The hazard is to allow imagined, habitual perceptions to become obstacles to the attainment of your dreams

Defy inertia. You will find no comfort in an obstacle. So, staying there, and thereby not dealing with it, is not an option.

Be carefully cautious with the exercise of a fear response. When faced with anxiety, ask yourself is it real? If so, escape the danger. If your fear is imagined, as it is most of the time, ask yourself: Why am I afraid? What am I afraid of?

Renowned operatic tenor, Enrich Caruso remedied his stage fright with positive self-talk. Instead of giving in to fear, he faced his anxiety by affirming his God-gifted ability to sing.

Determine the source of the fear stressors in your life. Use the How to Face Your Fear(s) exercise on the next page, it will teach you how to determine your fear source. After you have used this exercise, you will soon be able to categorize many of your fear triggers and quickly break-free of learned, habitual fear responses. You will make the necessary mental shifts so that harmful anxiety is released.

Mild anxiety is good. Oftentimes the "butterfly" tingle serves as a reminder of your expectation and ability to achieve. Repeated action repels fear. Fear not! Calm your fears. Believe and do.

Face each anxiety (fear) realistically. Devote more time to productive, calming activities such as meditation, prayer, songs, service to others, friendship chats, exercise, or group activities

Opportunity Step: Repeat: I am not new to this. I am true to this today.

Learn How to Face Your Fears

This exercise is designed to give you pause time to stop and objectively evaluate your fears. Be honest, the outcome depends on it. Repeat often until it becomes a first response habit.

1. Identify three of your greatest fears. Write them down.

2. Acknowledge each fear; say each one out loud using I am statements. (Example: I am afraid of ....)

3. For each fear write: Is it real or imagined. Be honest.

4. Educate yourself about each one. Re-write your script.

5. Write three affirmations you will use to overcome fear.

6. Set a definite goal to gradually eliminate each fear; i.e., public speaking for example, until you conquer it.

GOAL1:

GOAL2:

Obstacle 1:

Anger

"Anger is a wind which blows out the lamp of the mind."
—Robert G. Ingersoll

ANGER averts achievement. It is a wasted, perpetual emotion. Until you release inappropriate anger, progress is thwarted. However anger is appropriate in response to an injustice that needs to be righted. The achievement key is to release the anger once the situation or person has been confronted.

Embedded anger is costly; it can kill. Actually, anger harms the person who harbors it more than the one to which the anger is directed. Harriet Goldhor Lerner, in The Dance of Anger, writes, "use anger as a signal…to motivate us to say 'no' to the ways in which we are defined by others and 'yes' to the dictates of our inner self."

Examine your anger. Ask:
1. Who is my request of?
2. Has my request been spoken?
3. Is my request reasonable?

Anger is only one letter short of danger. Redirect your anger, stay out of danger. Focus on more beneficial conciliatory problem solving activities. Your success depends on it.

Stay calm.

Opportunity step: Use peaceful words/actions today.

Dr. Ben Carson in Gifted Hands openly describes his anger-filled youth, growing up in an impoverished inner-city Detroit neighborhood and the event that reversed his assumed destiny. He had been told he was headed for trouble; he would end up in jail or dead because of his violent temper. In spite of all that his mother did to divert him, he did not or could not control his anger until one day as he was fighting another boy with a knife in his hand, he realized that he could have killed his friend over a trivial matter. Nobly, Ben Carson got up and walked away and has never fought again. His instant awareness made all of the difference; he released the anger and began to grow.

After that incident, he was motivated to do his best. He attained college scholarships and attended medical school. Today, Ben Carson, M.D., is a world-renowned pediatric neurosurgeon recognized for separating conjoined twins and pioneering anti-seizure brain surgery.

Dr. Carson's secrets to success lie in his ability to channel anger into ways that better the health and spiritual well-being of others. "Why would God give us such a complex organ system unless He expects us to use it?", he asks.

How are you using your brain?

Obstacle 2:

Anxiety

"I know God won't give me anything I can't handle.
I just wish He didn't trust me so much."

—Mother Teresa

ANXIETY argues with logic. It is a by-product of undue worry, fear, and distrust in self-ability. Anxiety indicates a feeling of a loss of control which usually provokes a response to play it safe.

Don't play it safe. Playing it safe only retards success. Taking risks oftentimes evoke anxiety. Take the risk anyway. Pursue your dreams free-of-anxiety. Be free!

You can compress anxiety by:
- maintaining a positive attitude
- minimizing fear "talk"
- focusing on the present
- knowing your options

Following this blueprint will enable you to build trust in yourself so that you won't automatically regress. Interestingly, you'll often discover that the situation you were anxious about is not as dreadful as you had imagined

Have confidence.

Opportunity Step: Relax. Spend time in a garden or park today.

Behold the turtle.
He only makes progress
when he sticks his neck out.

—James Bryant Conant

Obstacle 3:

Apathy

"Most of us live as if we are homeless, we don't know our 'self' residence"

—Unknown

APATHY arrests growth. It is a neutral emotion. An apathetic person is breathing, thinking, and functioning but is not living with passion. Subconsciously, he feels that there is nothing he can do about life.

Optimism averts apathy. Be optimistic; it's essential to success. Some optimistic people know their success route early in life while others relinquish apathy and become optimistic when they are compelled to self-identify with an issue or cause after a harsh or catastrophic event.

Take for instance, MADD – Mothers Against Drunk Drivers. After her child was killed by a drunk driver, one mother began a campaign to enact state and federal laws that toughened jail sentences for drunk drivers. This movement, born out of one mother's pain, mobilized other mothers and other sympathizers. Today, MADD's lobbyist clout now impacts national agendas.

Do something.

Opportunity Step: Get involved! Join a club or group today.

The story of Vernon Damhler, a Mississippi store owner, who regis-
tered Blacks to vote, is about a man and his family who took a stand
in spite of the threat of death.

On January 12, 1966 Vernon Damhler was murdered and his home
and store property was burned by the white knights of the Mississippi
Ku Klux Klan because he stood against Jim Crow laws that enslaved
his people even though they were legally deemed free. His wife and
family were left with nothing but the indelible stamp of Vernon's conviction. It's ironic that four of his sons were enlisted men in the armed
forces fighting for freedom and justice abroad at the time of his
murder.

Sometimes it requires taking risks to fight apathy. It may mean that
your comfort is disturbed, your life is disarranged, or your mind is
awakened so that purposeful conviction can be born.

The Damhler family continues to tell their story so that all people in
the state of Mississippi can vote as free citizens.

Stand up, get involved. Act. Act now and continuously act.

Obstacle 4:

Appearances

"Were we to take as much pain to be what we ought, as we do to disguise what we are, we might appear like ourselves without being at the trouble of any disguise at all."

—Francois de la Rochefougauld

Appearances activate assumptions. Many people make instant decisions about one's worth based on appearances. In societies where materialism is rampant, appearances matter. Rather, a better indicator of worth is how well you have lived: Who have you helped? What have you contributed?

If you feel compelled to try to impress others with the latest gadget, mansion style houses, the latest model of expensive car, or with the voguest fashion even though you cannot afford either luxury, then appearance is an obstacle. Purchasing based on low self-esteem insecurity, indicates deeper inner problems. Beyond that, each month that you cannot pay the bills generated from buying these things—cars, clothes, gadgets, houses—unnecessary anxiety is created. Restrain the impulse to "buy for appearance sake" only. However, if you must purchase, let it be deliberate rather than impulsive gratification.

Build your wealth from within. Prestige is vanity. Don't try to "keep up with the Jones". At the end of each day, the only thing that matters is how many deposits you make into your success account.

Bank on your success.

Opportunity Step: Dispense appearances concerns today

Sam Walton, the founder of the booming enterprise Wal-Mart drove an old truck, lived in a modest home, and wore clothes sold in his stores until he died. Others looking at just his appearance, could have mistakenly pre-judged that he was a man of little means who could be ignored or labeled a "loser".

Sam Walton knew the folly of trying to keep up with the Jones'. Unlike Mrs. Bucket, on the British Comedy sitcom Keeping Up Appearances that mocks snobbery, Mr. Walton lived modestly.

It is a given that the value of a dollar is the same for everyone in a country at the same given time. It's what you do with the dollar that makes the difference. If you have a consumer mentality, then the dollar is for spending. If you have a saver mentality, a percentage of the dollar is saved or invested.

Life is like a coin. You can spend it any way you want, but you can only spend it once. Consider how you "spend" you life time. Grid out your patterns. If too much is invested in appearance, shift.

Be authentic.

Obstacle 5:

Arrogance

"The worst cliques are those which consist of one man."
—George Bernard Shaw

ARROGANCE atrophies success. It is only vain imagining. An arrogant person has convincingly deceived himself to believe that she or he needs no one and that they have all the answers. Actually, the extreme of confidence is arrogance. Any extreme is an obstacle because it indicates an out-of-balance perspective.

Arrogance often masks a deep insecurity. Insecurities such as: others may think I don't know the answer, that I am not good enough, or that I may not be accepted are combated by a persona of self-importance. Paradoxically, arrogance signals to those whose motive is to destroy or disrupt your dream, that you can be manipulated by pretentious flattery.

Whether you know enough, are good enough, or will be accepted is seldom the only determiner of success. Although knowledge is vital, confidence is more significant. Successful people associate with those who listen, care about others, and are willing to ask for help; the very things that an arrogant person find hard to do.

Be humble.

Opportunity step: Start writing a gratitude journal today.

In a Business Week article, "Class Act in the Valley," Linda Himelstein writes that Dan Case, brother of media magnate Steve Case, was a nice guy who lived an arrogant-free life. "At a time when business leaders inspire more scorn than esteem, Dan Case stands as a model of decency" she says.

Dan Case played a significant role in the industrialization of Silicon Valley. Himelstein adds "When Dan died at age 44 after a 15-month battle with brain cancer the world lost more than a good soul. It lost a man who serves as a reminder that Corporate America is populated by those who accomplish much good, not just by cheats and liars."

Dan Case was competitive, but never cut-throat. He was a risk-taker, but never dangerous. Dan case was powerful, but never arrogant. He was confident, but never prideful. He proved that nice guys do finish first.

Businesses need more executives who prefer the label "niceness". The drive to success need not be a bumper-car race.

> "There is nothing sexier than confidence."
> —Unknown

Obstacle 6:
Assumptions

"The greatest obstacle to discovery is not ignorance –
it is the illusion of knowledge."

—Daniel J. Boorstin

Assumptions annihilate truth. Many people have heard the saying, "assumptions make an ass out of you and me." Think about it. If you dissect the word assume, you will see ass-u-me. As crude as this may seem, the adage is true. Most assumptions are baseless.

Our minds quickly categorize situations based on previous history. It is oftentimes easier and safer to do so. This in turn makes the generalized assumptions you make easier to justify. But what if your assumptions are wrong? You could miss crucial opportunities.

To counterpoint, assumptions can also be correct. The past has its value, but one should seldom make quick assumptions based solely on the past. Instead, ponder what if? Pose questions. Fact-find. Once you do, your assumptions become a part of your truth.

Expand your vision. Question "your truth" sometimes. Probe for possibilities. Explore, look for latent potentialities. Discover a new model for your success.

Ask questions.

Opportunity Step: Investigate the validity of an assumption today

"The fountain of contentment must spring up in the mind,
and he who hath so little knowledge of human nature
as to seek happiness by changing anything
but his own disposition,
will waste his life in fruitless efforts
and multiply the grief process he purposes to remove.

—Samuel Johnson

Obstacle 7:

Attachment

"Attachment is the great fabricator of illusions; reality can be attained only by someone who is detached."

—Simon Weil

ATTACHMENT asphyxiates aspirations. Some people hold on to the status quo for so long and so hard that it chokes the life out of them and their dreams.

In the workplace, people become attached to office mates or a title. Others stay in damaging relationships even though they know it is best to move on. A majority of people stagnate because they are afraid to detach.

Attachments weave a secure safety net. But, in order to grow you have to learn to let go. Chopra, in The Seven Spiritual Laws of Success, says that "detachment does not mean you give up your intent and desires; you give up your attachment to the result." Thus, if you perpetuate held attachments out of fear, subconsciously you are affixed mentally to an outcome.

Un-stick yourself. Suspend your illusions and figure out what is your actual reality. Figure out what is best for you.

"It takes courage to grow up and turn out to be who you really are."

—e. e. cummings

Detach.

Opportunity Step: Learn a new skill or make a new friend today.

If you are not having fun – living your passion –
then change what you are doing or
how you are doing what you are doing.

There is no growth without change.

—Unknown

Obstacle 8:

Attitude

"An attitude of gratitude creates blessings."

—Sir John Templeton

Attitude amends achievement. One's state of mind is commensurate to the outcome one achieves in his life. A negative attitude effectuates poor results, whereas a positive attitude creates astounding results. The choice is yours.

Your internal viewpoint, what you really believe, is the basis of your attitude. If you exhibit an attitude of scarcity, fear, and mistrust this becomes your reality. Conversely, if you exhibit an attitude of sharing, love, and trust this formulates a sense of optimism. You are exactly what you believe.

If you believe that you can scale Mt. Everest, you can. If you believe you are limited according to the obstacles you face, then you are. Attitude is everything. The difference is only a matter of perspective and attitude.

Achievers have both an expectant attitude and gratitude. As you achieve, be grateful even for your challenges. Don't ask to move your obstacle, ask for the strength to climb. Affirm your capacity daily.

Be grateful.

Opportunity Step: Practice expressing your gratitude today.

"Do all the good you can,
by all the means you can,
in all the ways you can,
at all the times you can,
to all the people you can,
as long as you can...

—John Wesley

Obstacle 9:

Avarice

"Riches do not consist in the possession of treasures, but in the use made of them."

—Napoleon Bonaparte I

AVARICE ambushes riches. Avarice is the insatiable pursuit of or love of money. It is a selfish greed that ruins success.

Don't let money shortchange you. Parsimony or any extreme love that is unchecked is a cruel, powerful master. Paradoxically, the harder you pursue money, the more elusive it is. Yet, when you use money and its influence for the better good, it flows.

Giving to others is often a catalyst for greater bounty. But, giving need not always be monetary. It's often better if it is not. A gift could be an act of service for someone; i.e. babysitting for free, running errands for a senior citizen at no charge, or mowing the lawn for a neighbor who is ill. It even could be a compliment to a cashier, an apple to a teacher, or a hug for a friend.

Giving, not avarice, leads to riches. John McCormack in Self Made in America writes, "I can almost guarantee you that if your goal in life is to make money, it is almost certain that you never will.

Give and live richly.

Opportunity Step: Give something away today. IOU1.

Mark Victor Hansen, co-author of The One Minute Millionaire and The Chicken Soup series uses the analogy of the "Butterfly effect" to affect mental shifts.

His systematic approach to wealth attainment includes an altruistic component. Each One Minute Millionaire pledges the first 10% of their earning to serve humanity in order to make the world a better place.

The authors place emphasis on giving, rather than avarice (selfish) living as a cardinal principle of riches. Consider this syllogism:
- Giving feels good;
- Wealth is giving.
- Therefore, wealth is for good.

Avarice hurts. The aphorism, "No man becomes rich unless he enriches others" by Andrew Carnegie sums it up best.

Obstacle 10:

Backbiting

"Gossip is the art of saying nothing in a way that leaves practically nothing unsaid"

—Walter Winchell

Backbiting burns the heart. Backbiting (gossiping) minutely destroys both the listener and the gossiper. The temptation to gossip, or more softly, "share a secret", causes trust to be shattered.

Place yourself in the position of the person who is gossiped about and think about how you would feel if you were the object of malicious gossip. It doesn't feel good.

Passing on information about another, or backbiting, can be tamed by pledging to neither hear nor pass on gossip. It is a challenge to maintain a no gossip rule, especially since cultures and society seemingly endorses such. However, to see no evil, hear no evil nor speak no evil minimizes disagreements and fosters lasting, trusting relationships. Trust is critical to your success.

To speak ill of others is a dishonest way of praising ourselves.

—Will Durant

Praise instead of gossip and see how much better you feel. Compliment instead of verbally beating down another. Befriend instead of engaging in hurtful dialogue.

Praise.

Opportunity Step: Speak only kind, praiseworthy words today.

"Never say anything to hurt anyone.
Moreover…refrain from double talk,
From shrewd and canny remarks that are designed to advance
our interests at someone's disadvantage.
We are to turn our back upon evil, and in every
way possible, do good, help people
and bring blessings into their lives."

—Norman Vincent Peale

Obstacle 11:

Bitterness

"There are no justifiable resentments."

—Wayne Dyer

BITTERNESS bans happiness. Happiness and bitterness are irreconcilable opposites. One who is bitter is never happy. Whereas, one who is happy is never bitter.

Success is sweet. Winners use bitter experiences to their advantage as part of their motivation to excel. Like a winner, you too need not dwell on the unpleasant things of life. Instead, actively seek experiences that propel your greatness.

Bitterness is tart. Health problems, sour relationships, divorce, and deceit are all possible by-products of bitterness; it destroys happiness. Asperity weakens faith in yourself and your dreams; you need faith to achieve.

If you are bitter at heart, even success is not sweet. Suspend sharpness. Throw away resentments. The cost you pay for either is too high. There really are no justifiable resentments.

Banish bitterness.

Opportunity Step: Write a poem. Be happy today!

Bitterness imprisons life
LOVE RELEASES IT

Bitterness paralyzes life
LOVE EMPOWERS IT

Bitterness sickens life
LOVE HEALS IT

Bitterness blinds life
LOVE ANNOINTS ITS EYES

—Harry Emerson Fosidick
from Riverside Sermons

Obstacle 12:

Blame

"Self-pity is our worse enemy and if we yield to it, we can never do anything wise in the world."

—Helen Keller

BLAME bamboozles the mind. Projecting blame onto others for your fate or outcome is immature reasoning. Self-pity or blame takes away your chance to factor a solution. Thus, blame is a determinant of slow growth.

Contrary things happen; this is a maxim of life. Regardless of how hard you try, some challenges are beyond your control. To assign blame because of an altered outcome is shallow. Success is like a mirror; it reflects what you think and do. It is simple. Give the world blame and it is reflected back to you. Give the world your best and the best is reflected back to you.

If love makes the world go round, then blame stops it on its axis. Success definitely slows down when you resort to blame. Take responsibility, as tough as that may be, and move on. Don't adopt the role of a victim.

Blaming or wallowing in its self-pity is destructive. Move into your greatness. Step into your success. Live with courage and conviction. You will achieve.

Believe in your greatness.

Opportunity Step: Affirm yourself. Stop the blame today!

Louis Braille never blamed himself or others for his blindness. Instead, he used his physical challenge to "see" a solution. Little is known of Louis' life except that he grew up very poor in France and that he was plagued by ill health all of his life.

In 1812, at age 3, he was blinded while playing with an anvil in his father's saddle making shop. At the time, there were few services for the blind. At age ten his father sent him away to a school for blind children in Paris where they used an embossed alphabet reading, but not for writing.

Louis studied music there. He would become discouraged and run away only to return. Life on the streets of Paris was harsh for a little blind boy. His father, mother, and the school director died when he was 14. Now an orphan, he had little choice but to stay in school.

Mr. Braille heard about a system of night writing used by the French army that used punched holes in cardboard to communicate. Louis spent three years developing his own system for the blind which he presented to the Royal Academy, but was ignored. For twenty years he searched for support for his system. He died at age 43 still unsuccessful in the application of Braille still without blame. However now, Braille is used worldwide as a system of writing for the blind.

Obstacle 13:

Burnout

"The essential conditions of everything you do must be choice, love, passion."

—Nadia Boulanger

BURNOUT bend destiny.   Doing too much, at the sacrifice of your emotional and physical health, induces suffering. Burnout puts success on hold.

Prolonged stress and frustration are key causes of burnout. It is an indicator that your life areas are askew. Because of the frenetic pace that many people now live, burnout is so common that it is often overlooked as a lifestyle consequence. However, you can't climb any obstacle if you are exhausted. Re-energize.

Perfectionist and high achievers are the typical types who suffer from burnout. You don't have to push yourself to the limit to succeed. Achievers utilize coping mechanisms - relaxing, exercising, or a new hobby - so that they maintain a healthy, sustainable balance. Eliminate the rush.

It is important to have parts of your life that is not goal oriented.

Chill out.

Opportunity Step: Meditate for fifteen (15) minutes today.

Always bear in mind that your
own resolution to success is
more important than any other
one thing.

—Abraham Lincoln

Obstacle 14:
Calamity

"Expect troubles as an inevitable part of life, and when it comes, hold your head high. Look it squarely in the eye and say, "I will be bigger than you. You cannot defeat me."

—Ann Landers

Calamity cracks peace. Disorder can build both your confidence and your faith. While in the eye of the storm, calamities may not appear to be blessings in disguise, yet in many regards calamity is providence.

The Japanese Seicho-No-Ie movement uses the practice of choice to teach immunity from calamity. The premise is that it is how you exercise choice which restores one's balance. However, without practice, it is difficult to remember that you have choices when confronted with adversity.

You can choose to either see calamity as an eye opening chance to make empowering changes in your life or you may choose to see devastation and give up. The latter viewpoint is the response of a "victim" mindset while the former is that of one who sees "victory".

Winners always choose victory.

Decide.

Opportunity Step: Count your choices for an hour today.

There is no chance,
no destiny,
or no fate,
that can circumvent
or hinder,
or control
the firm resolve of a
determined soul

—Ella Wheeler Wilcox

Obstacle 15:
Change

"Growth cannot happen without change."

—Unknown

Change challenges complacency. Variation compels movement. Therefore, change is good especially if it spurs you to act. Embrace change as you pursue success.

Live your life in a deliberate, active motion. Second by second, minute by minute, hour by hour, day by day, month by month, year by year—change is a life constant. Even so, changes should never distract the focus you must have in order to attain your goals. Flexibility should be embedded in every process and goal so that you can respond and adjust.

Stephen Covey says "begin with the end in mind" which implies that regardless of whatever changes, you fixate on the end result. Then, an inevitable change will not thwart your purpose.

Learn to go with the flow. Be amenable to change so that you adeptly adapt and maximize your potential. Your success depends on your ability to change.

"There is nothing permanent except change."   —Heraclitus

Accept change.

Opportunity Step: Initiate a change. Do something new today.

The mind has exactly the same
power as the hands, not merely to
grasp the world, but to change it.

—Colin Wilson

Obstacle 16:

Competitiveness

"Do what you can, with what you have, where you are."

—Theodore Roosevelt

COMPETITIVENESS competes with success. When competitiveness overrides the cannons of respect and decency, it debases ones greatness. Whether in sports or business, never overstep the boundary of propriety.

Success is competitive. From an external perspective there will always be newer, more innovative products, strategies, ideas, or services. Internally, man by nature is competitive. Pat Riley, one of the winningest professional basketball coaches in sports history, says winners know how to use external and innate competition to build a stronger team or success plan. In The Winner Within: A Life Plan for Team Players, Riley uses the principle of teamwork, rather than competition, as his pivot to inspire success in others.

A true winner is competitive, but not brutal. Learn how to compete so that you don't defeat your success. Plot your success so that you are known for your commitment to excellence, integrity, and willingness to be of service to others.

Play fair.

Opportunity Step: Play a game of chess today.

"Our business in life is not to get ahead of others,
but to get ahead of ourselves – to break our own records,
to outstrip our yesterday by our today."

—Stewart Johnson

Obstacle 17:

Complacency

"The greater danger is not that our hopes are too high and we fail to reach them, but that they are too low and still we do."
                                        —Michelangelo Buonarroth

COMPLACENCY corrodes continuity. Standing still will never get you to the finish line. Complacency is the death of success.

Joyce Brown in Getting Unstuck advises the practice of visualization to activate action. Another practice that she promotes is to make a daily goals list or a detailed personal master plan.

Sometimes people lapse into periods of complacency because of burnout. But, a focus on the future and the creativity of discovering new solutions often precipitates life altering breakthroughs. If you are experiencing chronic complacency, seek help; this may signal depression.

Activity combats complacency. Do something. Think creatively. Plan in detail; listing out daily tasks and projections for the future. Write down your success goals in a timeline every day.

> You miss 100% of the shots you never take.
>   —Wayne Gretzky

Energize.

Opportunity Step: Make a new list of goals today.

I HOPE YOU DANCE
Willie Brooks Williams

Obstacle 18:

Complaining

"Gratitude is riches. Complaining is poverty. Instead of complaining about what is wrong, be grateful for what is right."

—Unknown

COMPLAINING clogs the soul. The old adage "There's no use in complaining, nobody wants to hear it anyway" is still true. There is no use complaining as long as you have options to explore. Manage your options until you succeed.

Refrain so that you won't become known as a habitual complainer. Instead re-use that energy. Recast your focus so that your success is not sabotaged by your own negativity.

Examine your mindset. If negativity spews out automatically, it is time for an attitude check-up. Complaining is oftentimes triggered by fear. Address it. Look deep within yourself to find its root and pluck it out.

Turn your fears into cheers. Be optimistic rather than finding fault. Believe in your ability to make things happen.

Be grateful, not hateful.

Opportunity step: Smile all day long. Spread some cheer today.

If you do not like something, change it.
If you can't change it, change your
attitude. Don't complain.

—Maya Angelou

Obstacle 19:

Conceit

"Conceit. God's gift to little men."

—Bruce Barton

CONCEIT crushes companionship. No man stands alone, it is conceited to think so. Everyone relies on someone at one time or another. Acknowledge those who have contributed to your success.

No one succeeds alone. There are truly no entirely self-made men. Even though you may convincingly think that you made it entirely on your own, it is not true. No matter what you achieve, somebody has helped you. A winner is humble enough to say thank you.

Let your focus be outward rather than inward. An inward angle is vain; but an outward angle reflects you and others. Conceit fosters a selfish small mindedness. John Ruskin attests that "conceit may puff a man up, but will never prop him up."

Minimal mind, minimal outcome. Maximized mind, expanded outcome. It doesn't matter how strong, agile, or competent you are, you have been supported and have needed the support of others. People need people.

Say thank you.

Opportunity Step: Send a thank you note to three people today.

Instead of seeing just me,
I see a world of opportunity.

-Unknown

Obstacle 20:

Conflict

"Why can't we all get along?"

—Rodney King

CONFLICT confounds destiny. Pernicious conflict is destructive. But cooperation is productive. Winning is not a battle of wills, it takes cooperation to succeed.

Life is not a contest. The equation conflict equals contest instigates unrest. This form of competition breaks down understanding. However, when deliberate steps are taken to bridge understanding, commonalities emerge. A sense of empathy is of incalculable value to your success.

Conflict, of any form, is resolvable. Even though you aspire to win, agreements can be brokered where both parties win. It is how you perceive the outcome that makes the difference.

Conflict is not inevitable. When you make sure your needs are known, you avert debate and discord. Cooperation is peaceful.

Practice peace.

Opportunity Step: Use "I need" statements today.

"You must choose between making money
and making sense.
The two are mutually exclusive."

—Richard Buckminister Fuller

Obstacle 21:

Contentment

"A man who is contented with what he has done will never become famous for what we will do."

—Nicholas Boleau

CONTENTMENT conserves energy. After you have done all you can, soared as high as possible, and achieved your best, you deserve the right to say "I am content" and really mean it.

However, if you are falsely saying that you are content, you are actually creating a myriad of other obstacles. Often just below the surface in your subconscious the truth torments you. Obesity, depression, excuses, blaming, migraines, and unfinished projects are escapisms that result from that inner deception.

You can't fool mother life. Regardless of how well you coach yourself or project contentedness, you can fake it but for so long. But, you can find peaceful contentment by living authentically.

Release pretension. Be authentic in everything you do. Have enough courage to tell yourself first and then others the truth. Forgo the vanity of faking it. Own up to your messes so that when you say you are content, it is really true.

Carpe diem.

Opportunity Step: Only say yes when you really want to today.

Being "contended" ought to mean in English,
as it does in French, being pleased.
Being content with an attic ought not to
mean being unable to move from it and
resigned to living in it:
it ought to mean appreciating all
there is in such a position.
For true contentment is a real,
even an active virtue – not only affirmative
but creative.
It is the power of getting out of any situation
all there is in it.

Miscellany of Men
—G. K. Chesterton

Obstacle 22:

Control

"Act as if what you do makes a difference. It does.

—Robin Williams

CONTROL chokes success. For many, control means power. What an illusion. Power and control are, and should be, distinct.

The old paradigm of business operation and leadership taught toughness and control as its cornerstone. Today's management thought anchors the "we" mentality as integral to success.

Personal success too is a process of sharing rather than one of control. The need to control is really based on fear. And, a principal sense of fear destroys the attainment of success.

You get better results with trust and cooperation. Better results are based on better decision making. Better decision making happens when honest input is valued. Form a mastermind group. Learn how to express your needs, expose your weaknesses, and build a base of support. Control equals power only when it is shared.

"Would you rather be right or happy?"
—Jerry Jampolsky

Relax.

Opportunity Step: Have an "I am not in charge" day today.

Dorothy Maric, author of Managing With the Wisdom of Love, is current with new, more inclusive, management trends. She identified five management virtues in her book.

The virtues are:
1. Trustworthiness
2. Unity
3. Respect and dignity
4. Justice
5. Service and humility

These once unheralded management virtues are now entrenched in successful organizational culture because of the impact they add to an organization's profitability.

Although these virtues are slanted toward organizations and businesses, it takes the same virtue pool to achieve personal success. Virtue is a success fundamental.

One virtue at a time, one relationship at a time. One virtue at a time, more success over time.

Obstacle 23:

Criticism

"Sandwich every bit of criticism between two layers of praise."

—Mary K. Ash

CRITICISM creates crises. Nothing kills hope faster than criticism. Look inward, the only permissible criticism is to negativity within you.

Caustic words wound. The acidic nature of a critical tongue has the potential to breakdown the staunchest optimist. Realistically, not everything someone does is laudable. But, champions know how to affirm others through the use of constructive feedback.

The tendency to criticize and then apologize is damaging. This pattern is so standardized today that it seems almost reflexive. Something is wrong with this cycle. Don't apologize if your words were thoughtfully spoken as a reality check. Offer your corrections along with examples or suggestions for improvement and be sure to acknowledge that which is good. Seek or give feedback, shun criticism.

Criticism is harsh. Try a new approach that invests in praise. Look for the good. Use a modest tongue. Any situation is correctable. The best solution is governed by its tone.

Praise.

Opportunity Step: Practice using praise today.

Children Learn What They Live

If a child lives with criticism; he learns to condemn.
If a child lives with hostility; he learns to fight.
If a child lives with ridicule; he learns to be shy.
If a child lives with shame, he learns to feel guilty.
If a child lives with tolerance, he learns to be patient.
If a child lives with encouragement, he learns confidence.
If a child lives with praise, he learns to appreciate.
If a child lives with fairness, he learns justice.
If a child lives with security, he learns to have faith.
If a child lives with approval, he learns to like himself.
If a child lives with acceptance and friendship,
He learns to find love in the world.

—Dorothy Law Nolte, 1963

Obstacle 24:

Cynicism

"Cynicism is nothing but idealism gone sour in the face of frustration."

—Bruell G. Gallagher

Cynicism cuts down hope. It is the bane of progress. A cynic is a fear-filled snob who projects onto others what they cannot accept about themselves. Victors change what they don't like and accept what they can't change.

Be confident. Believe 100% that you will achieve. Stop bending to cynicism; instead get in the game. Take risks, even make a few mistakes. Your dream is not so fragile. It will not break. Never give up in despair, always have hope.

Forgive failures instead of sinking into a drowning pool of cynicism. Anyone who achieves has failed. Get on with your life's work. Forgo the negative. Allow no time for complaining. Life is painful enough and achieving success is grueling enough.

Laugh more. Smile too. Don't forget to sprinkle a little compassion on your tongue; say a kind word or two.

Enjoy.

Opportunity step: Write down your dreams down today.

Four things come not back:
The cynical word,
The sped arrow,
The past life
The neglected opportunity

—Arabian Proverb

Obstacle 25:

Debt

"Debt and misery live on the same road."

—Russian Proverb

DEBT destroys wealth. The lack of financial discipline is its primary cause. Even if you need to acquire debt to pursue your dream, do so methodically.

Do nothing in haste. If you cede to pressure believing in a deal that's too good to be true, the risk is usually too high. Oftentimes, you end up making a costly mistake. Research any financial decisions first. Take your time.

Manage your debt. You are out of control when you rob Peter to pay Paul or when you lie to creditors when they call seeking payment. If you are nearing or in this place, it is time to create a debt-free plan.

Take deliberate, concrete steps to change your debt behavior.
- **Stop** purchasing. Go on a spending fast.
- **Start** a debt diet. Cut out impulsive purchases.
- **Set** financial goals. Save more than you spend.

Use the 3S process to begin debt success. Stop. Start. Set.

You can't buy success.

Opportunity Step: Go to a free, no cost, event today.

Jane Bryant Quinn, respected financial guru and author of Making the Most of Your Money, advises to take charge of your money. She says, have a spending plan. "That's the only way to coerce your money into doing what you really want. A spending plan is an "active strategy for getting wherever you want to go", Quinn adds.

A spending plan, like goals, must be written down and it must have specific markers identifying definite timeliness to reflect how well you are accomplishing each financial goal.

Financier Quinn tells the reader to write down all cash expenditures for a month. Day by day record what you spent. Secondly, she advises to audit your checkbook and bank card statements for the past six months. Itemize these expenses into categories. Next, construct a spending chart. She says this snapshot may surprise you. "It is not unusual to discover that you are better off than you thought. Fear often arises from ignorance."

Know your spending habits. Save more than you spend on a regular basis. Stop impulsive buying. Set financial goals and stick to them

Pay yourself first.

Obstacle 26:

Denial

"Truth is like the sun. You can shut it out for a time, but it ain't going away."

—Elvis Presley

DENIAL decimates reality. It delays progress because you are not operating in the present. You can attempt to deny reality, but sooner or later you will be forced to take an accurate, honest look at where you are, who you are, and how you are living.

The truth reaper will visit you even in the land of denial. To achieve success you must take a realistic snapshot of your life. Ask yourself vital questions that others may not have the courage to ask. Ask yourself:

Say, Self –
- What do I value?
- Who are my friends, associates?
- Why am I ...?
- Where am I going?
- What do I need to change?

Destiny is a place you work to get to. You'll never get there by living in de-nile. Come out of the river.

Deny, denial

Opportunity step: Answer the above five questions today.

MYSELF

I have to live with myself,
and so I want to be fit for myself to know; I want to be able as days
go by always to look myself straight in the eye.

I don't want to stand with the setting sun
and hate myself for the things I have done.
I don't want to keep on a closet shelf a lot of secrets about myself
and fool myself as I come and go
into thinking nobody else will know
the kind of man I really am;
I don't want to dress me up in a sham.

I want to go out with my head erect;
I want to deserve all men's respect;
But here in the struggle for fame and pelf,
I want to be able to like myself.
I don't want to think as
I come and go that I'm bluster and bluff and empty show.

I can never hide myself from me,
I see what others can never see.
I know what others may never know –
I can never fool myself – and so,
whatever happens, I want to be self-respecting
And conscience free.
                    —Edgar A. Guest

Obstacle 27:

Depression

"We either make ourselves happy or miserable. The result is the same."

—Carlos Casteneda

DEPRESSION debates with reality. Emotional pain, caused by depression, distorts reality and one's perception of self-worth. A healthy valuation of one's worth is vital to success.

Hyper criticalness, low spirits, irritability, lack of motivation, inability to concentrate and reluctance to take on even simple tasks are common symptoms of depression. Have hope, depression is treatable.

Catastrophic events threaten one's stability and even shuffle one's values and priorities. But, withstanding a catastrophe, many people live at such a frenzied pace their emotional stability may be threatened. Inner anxiety and other stressors eventually zap your vitality and soon your quality of life suffers.

Don't worry, be happy. One of the first courses of action is to turn on hope. Tap into happiness. Tune into your goals and needs. Exercise. Begin to practive yoga or participate in a recreational sport. Do something. Increase your energy.

Be encouraged.

Opportunity Step: Laugh more today.

Andrew Solomon, author of The Noonday Demon: An Atlas of Depression, candidly explores the subject. He courageously exposes his own bout with emotional pain so that others will understand the experience of a breakdown.

Solomon studied at Yale University and the Jesuit College in Cambridge, England. He was a writer for The New Yorker, The New York Times Magazine and ArtForm. His depression emerged "when life was finally in order and all the excuses for the pain had been used up", he says.

Depression, a treatable disease, robs your senses of purpose. It creates panic, health problems, anxiety, poor decision-making, and other challenging frailties.

With proper medical therapy, Solomon stabilized and now lives filled with hope. He says the adversity of depression makes him "look deeper at life…. I cannot find it in me to regret entirely the course my life has taken. Everyday I choose, sometimes gamely and sometimes against the moment's reason, to be alive. Is that not a rare joy?"

Obstacle 28:

Despair

"Hope begins in the dark, the stubborn hope that if you just show up and try to do the right thing, the dawn will come. You wait and watch and work: You don't give up."

—Anne Lamont

DESPAIR delays dreams. Feelings of hopelessness, that despair precipitates, can cause you to abandon your dreams. Don't do it. Dream on!

Success starts with an unshakable belief in your dreams. Joy gives wings to every dream. Don't despair. Find your joy. Sometimes a change in perspective such as seeing the glass half full will make all the difference. Finding joy may also mean making changes in your life. Whatever if takes, begin sleuthing now. Banish despair and soar.

Action activates dreams. Activity banishes despair. Do away with unhealthy habits. Start a new hobby. Take a walk in the park. Get busy, life awaits you. Embrace life. Don't despair. Believe in yourself and in your dreams. Transform your life for the better.

Write down new ideas or goals. Concentrate on your success. There is nothing better you can do. Focus your power on inventing your greatness.

Get busy!

Opportunity step: Draw a bridge scene today.

A small trouble is like a pebble.
Hold it too close to your eyes and
it fills the whole world
and puts everything out of focus.

Hold it at a proper distance
and it can be examined
and properly classified.

Throw it at your feet
and it can be seen in its true setting,
just one more tiny bump
on the pathway of life.

Cecilia Lace

Obstacle 29:
Destiny

"Choice, not chance, will determine our ultimate destiny"

—Anonymous

DESTINY deports choice. Destiny is not always a destination. Glen Bland writes, "Success is the progressive realization of predetermined goals stabilized with balance and purified by belief." No one is destined to succeed without the ethos of work.

Do you know someone who was "destined" to be a singer, artist, teacher, speaker, doctor, attorney, skater, sports player or mechanic? What usually goes unmentioned is what these "destined" people had to sacrifice in order to reach their destiny.

You are uniquely created for greatness. Some quickly make it to the summit while others experience setbacks, tragedy, or disappointments along the way. But, sadly there are only a few in the latter group who persevere until they too make it to the top.

> The miracle power that elevates the few is to be found in their industry, application and perseverance, under the promptings of a brave determined spirit.
>
> —Mark Twain

Destiny. Choice. It's up to you, only you can decide.

Opportunity step: Make a different choice today.

Destiny is not a matter of chance,
it is a matter of choice;
it is not a thing to be waited for,
it is the thing to be achieved.

-William Jennings Bryant

Obstacle 30:
Disability

"The only disability in life is a bad attitude."

—Scott Hamilton

DISABILITY distends success. In the world of success, only the strong survive. You must have a strong attitude, a strong conviction, and a strong character to preserve to the end.

If your mind cannot see possibilities, then you are disabled. Mental debilitation is the most formidable disability. Its remedy is increased fervor. You can pursue and achieve anything that your mind can conceive. Your mind doesn't recognize disability.

On July 4th the wheelchair competitors in Atlanta's Peachtree Road Race electrify the crowd. Up and down the Peachtree Street sidewalk, you hear shouts, "You can make it", "Don't give up", "Push, push, push" cheering them on. Visualize your own race.

Cheer yourself on to victory. You can make it! Don't give up! Push, push, push harder and harder. You are a winner!

Mental attitude = aptitude.

Opportunity Step: Spread some cheer today.

Actor Christopher Reeve is not disabled even though he is confined in a wheelchair. Everyday he pushes himself; he believes he will walk again.

In 1995 Christopher Reeve fell from a horse while riding and was pronounced permanently disabled as a paraplegic. Although he had a broken spine, the superman actor vowed he would beat the odds. It looks like he has.

Reeve describes his battle for mobility as a championship run for all people with spinal vertebrae injury. In spite of what he was told, he never succumbed to the predictable medical prognosis. From his hospital bed he mouthed to his wife, "I will walk again."

Reeve has resumed his movie career, acting and directing on and off screen. He uses his celebrity status to raise international interest about spinal cord injury and to raise money for a cure.

Reeve is superman. He is a super man who has tenacious belief.

What you believe, you can achieve.

Obstacle 31:
Disbelief

"I believe I can fly."

—R. Kelly

DISBELIEF depreciates dreams. It throttles success and short-stops progress. Believe. You are exactly what you believe.

Disbelief is self-defeating. Nothing makes you feel worse and nothing atrophies a dream faster. However, few things are more gratifying than overcoming disbelief. You have to believe to the end. Les Brown says it's not over until you win it!

Dr. Mark Goldston, in his book Get Out of Your Own Way – Overcoming Self-Defeating Behavior asserts that disbelief is a coping mechanism created by fear. He adds that your mindset determines your outcome. He says "If you want success, the path to it begins with what you believe about your ability to achieve."

If you don't believe in you who will? Believe in your capacity. Accept no defeat. Break through boundaries. Dream grandiosely for belief formulates your destiny.

"Dream like a fool."   —Bishop T. D. Jakes

Believe.

Opportunity step: Use "I Can" statements today.

Emerald farmer, Jamie Hill, was a believer even when others called him crazy. Undaunted, Hill kept on digging. Even when his family refused to loan him the money to buy acres of land for him to prospect, Hill secured a bank loan and kept on digging.

After 11 years of mining in the foothills of North Carolina, on Thanksgiving Day 1998, Jamie Hill hit pay dirt. North Carolina emeralds that is, he hit the mother lode.

Within a few days, the miner unearthed more than 3,000 carats of pristine emeralds. In jest, Hill calls his lode trail The Yellow Brick Road to Emerald City.

Hill's dream paid off. He did not allow disbelief in himself to halt his known passion. Disbelief could have seeped in when Hill was more than $200,000 in debt or when he was only days away from having his equipment and truck repossessed, but he never allowed such.

Hill kept on believing. Like Hill, so can you.

Keep on digging.

Obstacle 32:

Disease

"Diseases of the soul are more dangerous and more numerous than those of the body."

—Cicero

DISEASE deepens dreams. Its amazing how the immune systems in the body reacts when a disease is present. Lymph and garrisons of antibodies attack the invader.

Activate your dream defense system. Although a diseased mental attitude is not subject to biological attack, it should be. Low self-esteem, fear, disbelief is often far worse than any bodily disease

The antibiotic for mental disease is conviction. You have to vigorously attack mental blockages. A combination dose of hope, happiness, and healthy habits vitamins is an antitoxin. Fill your mind with this 3H remedy and refill this mental disease fighting prescription often.

Become your own success doctor. Do frequent "check ups from the neck up". Exude positive belief. Strengthen your bad attitude immunity. Attack an attitude of defeat. Increase your hope, happiness, and healthy habits.

Be optimistic.

Opportunity step: Volunteer at a senior center today.

Dr. Joseph Murray, author of The Miracle of Mind Dynamics: A New Way to Triumphant Living and The Power of Your Subconscious Mind, writes that you can be well and stay well.

An immutable law of life is belief. As you believe, you manifest. Dr. Murray believes that man is what he thinks about all day long, and that character is the totality of his thinking. He says:

> In order to experience good luck or good fortune,
> realize you are the master of your thoughts, emotions,
> and reactions to life. You are the maker and
> shaper of your conditions, experiences, and events.
> Every thought felt as true, or allowed to be accepted
> as true by your conscious mind, takes root in your
> subconscious mind.

You are what you believe. Garbage in, garbage out. Serenity in, serenity out. Compassion in, compassion out.

You have infinite riches within your reach. ...all you have to do is open your mental eyes and behold the treasury of infinity within.

Obstacle 33:

Distrust

"At the gate where suspicion enters, love goes out."

—Thomas Fuller

DISTRUST devalues progress. Cynicism operates in the fertile ground of distrust. The more you lack trust in others, the more your own progress is retarded.

Hope is the fulcrum of success. It is the staff of life. Hal Lindsey says "Man can live for about 40 days without food, and about three days without water, about eight minutes without air...but only one second without hope." Enliven your hope.

A spirit of hope emerges when you trust others. When you distrust, you are emotionally disengaged. Temper distrust. Its viscous cycle of suspicion is ameliorated when there is love, hope, and joy.

Believe. Have faith. Self-trust is the first secret of success. Another secret is to trust others. Cultivate a discerning trust in others. Trust and be trusted. To trust is the healthy thing to do.

Increase your trust.

Opportunity Step: Go out and lean on a tree today.

Just trust yourself, then you will
know how to live.

—Johann Wolfgang von Goethe

Obstacle 34:
Divorce

The chief cause of divorce is matrimony.

—Unknown

DIVORCE distances the heart. Divorce happens! In America nearly half of all couples who marry will end up as divorcees. Yet, women and men still fall in love every day.

Divorce, or any breakup, is not an excuse to become stuck. It is debilitating to blame him or her no matter how much you hurt. Remove the bitterness. Take time to heal and restore trust in your ability to make lasting love connections from your heart.

There are many lessons to learn from the experience of divorce. Quickly learn the lesson, objectively examine your role. Before you begin any relationship, identify what pleases you in a mate. Make a checklist of your ideal traits. If someone you meet does not meet the minimal criteria, recognize that and move on.

You can't hurry love.

"The virtue of the candle is not in the wax that leaves its trace, but in its light." — Antione de Saint-Exupery

Release.

Opportunity Step: Pluck a daisy today.

I will survive

—Gloria Gaynor

Obstacle 35:

Doubt

"Doubt is not a pleasant condition, but it certainly is an absurd one."

—Voltaire

DOUBT destroys dreams. A dream deferred because of doubt eventually becomes a vague longing. The foundation of all dreams is belief and conviction. The cornerstone of a dream is desire. The undergirding of desire is faith.

Unmatched belief in your dreams is the certainty you will need to follow through to your success. Steven Leidell, in The Extraordinary Nature of Ordinary Things, espouses that all dreams can come true, if you believe.

Napoleon Hill (1883-1970) says "You are searching for the magic key that will unlock the door to the source of power and yet you have the key in your own hands, and you may use it the moment you learn to control your own thoughts." Never doubt.

If you really believe, you will succeed. You are born with all the talent and faculties to do so. The power of greatness is within. Faith in your ability, even the size of a mustard seed, is a must.

Destroy doubt.

Opportunity Step: Write "I believe" statements today.

If you think you are beaten, you are.
If you think you dare not, you don't.
If you'd like to win but think you can't,
It's almost certain that you won't.
Life's battles don't always go
To the stronger woman or man,
But sooner or later, those who win
Are those who think they can.

—Author Unknown

Obstacle 36:
Emulation

"Emulation lives so near to envy that it is sometimes difficult to establish the boundary lines."

—Henry Giles

EMULATION erases self-identity. To want to be like Mike, Mary or Martin is commendable. But never emulate anyone to such a degree that the real you is forsaken. Get real!

Get real by removing any layers of false pretense. Be courageous enough to know and let others know the real you. One way to safeguard against total emulation is to examine yourself. Create a self-identity snapshot. Ask:
- Who am I?
- What do I like?
- What makes me happy?
- Where am I going?
- Why am I me?

Know your own face first.

"If I try to be like him, who will be me." (Yiddish proverb)

Be yourself.

Opportunity step: Answer the above five questions today.

The life which is unexamined is not worth living.

—Socrates

Obstacle 37:

Envy

"He who envies admits his inferiority."

—Latin Proverb

ENVY eviscerates life. The moment envy begins to fester is the moment when success wanes away. You are not inferior. You are already equipped for greatness. There is no reason for you to envy another.

You have within you everything you need to succeed. Dream big. Make concrete goals. Work until you triumph.

Envy never fulfills dreams. Insecurity or feelings of inferiority never marches over obstacles. Only persistent effort, a determined mind, and an inviolable self-assurance overcome obstacles so that dreams come true. Work hard and concentrate intensely on your dream. Never covet someone else's success. Sweat and toil; create your own.

"To fulfill a dream, to be allowed to sweat over lonely labor, to be given the chance to create, are the meat and potatoes of life."

—Bette Davis

Erase envy.

Opportunity Step: Do a kind act of service today.

He who wants a rose,
must first respect a thorn.

—Persian Proverb

Obstacle 38:

Equivocation

"Success isn't magic or hocus-pocus. It's simply learning how to focus."

—Mark Victor Hansen

EQUIVOCATION exploits choice. Are you like the Mad Hatter, always running around, indecisive and hyper, actually doing nothing? Or do you drive others mad because it takes you too long to decide?

Successful people are not equivocators. Winners decisively take risks. Champions weigh the consequences and then choose. Deliberateness, not evasion, is a mark of success.

Make fact-based decisions. Once a decision is made, forget about it. Don't analyze and fret over it. Instead, establish procedures and identify the resources you need in order to produce the outcome you expect. Focus your success lenses. See the solution as you begin, keep the end in view.

Decisiveness never produces ulcers but, equivocation can.

Decide.

Opportunity Step: Use "I have decided" statements today.

Better Decisions in Five Easy Steps

1. Determine the issues. Write a column of pro and con. List the possible benefits or consequences.

2. Review the list. Consult with others who may be neutral or passionate about the outcome.

3. Examine possibilities. Look at best practices, fact-find and analyze strategies.

4. Analyze consequences. Critically review whether the possibilities outweigh the consequences or vice versa.

5. Make a decision. Take action. Act as if the desired outcome has already happened. Live with the bold assurance that your decision has been confirmed and you are on your guided path.

Obstacle 39:

Excuses

"To defend yourself for your fault is to commit another fault"

—Italian Proverb

EXCUSES evaporate energy. They soon zap your plan of success. If you are not careful, excuses will instigate stagnation.

Excuses interest no one except your competition. The words: "I know, but", "But", "If only", "When", or "Because" appended to a reasoning is an excuse no matter how honest it is. If it looks like an excuse, acts like an excuse, or sounds like an excuse, wake up, it's an excuse.

Stop making excuses. Plan better. Start creating a plan by writing down your goal(s) every day. As part of your planning strategy: determine who you need to contact, what research you need to complete, and what tasks need to be done.

In The Four Agreements excuses are combated another way. The author, Don Miguel Ruiz, decrees that we must deliberately:
1. Be impeccable with your word
2. Don't take anything personally
3. Don't make assumptions
4. Always do your best

Agree to no more excuses.

Opportunity Step: Practice The Four Agreements today.

Only those who will risk going too far
can possibly find out how far one can go

—T. S. Elliot

Obstacle 40:

Family

"Every man is born into the world to do something unique
and distinctive. If he does not do it, it will never be done."

—Benjamin E. Mays

FAMILY fences hope. For many, nothing or no one is more important than family. For others, this is not the case. Regardless, family
matters. However, even with the best intention, an over dependence
on family can thwart your ambitions.

There is nothing safer than a supportive family unit. But, family
reliance is a challenge if you await permission or approval before you
make a decision. Soliciting the advice of loved ones is a sound practice. Even so, never relinquish your responsibility to pursue your
unique destiny, independent of family history.

Family advice is valuable; it shapes part of your identity. As with any
his-story, you have to add to the "story" so that you make your imprint
in such a way that it supplements your formative, familial identity.
You are not a carbon copy of anyone else.

Focus on the winner in you. Whatever your history, travel your own
path of success. Become who you need to be. Family or not, you
must pursue your dreams. Fulfill your destiny.

Be.

Opportunity Step: Tell a family member your dreams today.

Chinese immigrant, Chi Chang, grew up in a home of proud, educated family members. His father, an emigrate from China, attended Yale on a Fulbright scholarship and Harvard medical school. Chi followed his father's tradition, attending Yale University himself. As a pre-med student he noticed the poor people living next door to the posh campus.

He saw the under served children and felt compelled to volunteer in an after-school program. Chi found his destiny.

His father turned his back on him, refusing to support him. Chi, determined to follow his heart, lived in a housing project and on food stamps for a year. He also thought often of the Chinese children still living in China who were so poor their survival hinged on charity from day to day. He says, "This made me realize how lucky I am".

Today, Chi dedicates his life to encouraging children as a teacher at the Boston Academy of the Pacific Realm. He found his own path in a job that "imparts life."

(Extracted from an episode on the Oprah Winfrey Show)

Obstacle 41:
Fortune

"Fortune favors the bold."

—Virgil

FORTUNE filters conviction. Money, or the lack thereof, is an enabler. Many perceive the rich as elites who are "born with a silver spoon in their mouth". Sometimes the rich have it easier; sometimes riches are a curse.

Success requires conviction, whether you are rich or not. It's a true fortune that everybody has. A lack of money does not consign you to poverty, but a lack of aspiration does. There is no economic status attached to a dream. Annals are replete with stories about everyday people who achieved greatness even though they were impoverished at the beginning.

Achievement can't be bought. It takes effort and drive to achieve any dream. There are few success shortcuts. Add boldness to your fortune chest.

Fortune is a cushion, just watch out for the pins.

Be Bold.

Opportunity Step: Spend time with a waiter today.

To succeed
you need to find something to hold on to,
something to motivate you,
something to inspire you.

—Tony Dorsett

Obstacle 42:

Friends

"Friends are angels who lift us to our feet when our wings
can no longer fly."

—Unknown

FRIENDS fertilize dreams. Make new friends, but keep the old.
One is silver and the other's gold. This old Girl Scout rhyme allows
you to distinguish relationships. Friends are either silver, gold, or old.

Friendships matter. Make new friends, but loose the toxic ones too.
Disallow draining relationships that siphon your success energy.
Negative, clinging friends become obstacles when they intrude upon
or impede your dreams.

Overreliance on the opinions of others stall success. It's sensible to
share your ideas with others for feedback. What better mastermind
than a friend who is courageous enough to add truthful input. What
is not good is a constant barrage of insipid negativity. Not all friendships are eternal.

If a friendship sours, move on. Don't hang on to outworn, draining
friendships out of obligation. Release them and yourself.

Soar.

Opportunity Step: Make a new friend today.

Friendship is always a sweet responsibility,
never an opportunity.

—Khalil Gibran

Obstacle 43:

Frustration

"The guy who takes a chance, who walks the line between the known and the unknown, who is unafraid of failure, will succeed."

—Gordon Parks

FRUSTRATION fuels doubt. It is easy to quit when you are frustrated. That's what losers do. Front runners never allow frustration to cloud their dream.

Decline the indulgence of frustration. Keep going. Go around the mountain if you have to until you find a straight narrow path to the summit. Never allow frustration to avert your focus. "Obstacles are those frightful things you see when you take your eyes off your goals" says Malcolm Forbes.

Be ever vigilant, never give up. Plow on, even though you are perplexed. The solution is nearby. It is aggravating to fail in spite of how often you repeat the process. Don't become frustrated and give up. Frustration is short-lived. Success is imminent at that point. Hold on, don't quit now.

Increase your passion. Be unafraid of failure. Re-fresh your achievement memory if you need too. Invite some friends over and host an "I remember when" party. Do whatever you need to do to convert frustration into avidity. You can't fail if you do.

Never give up.

Opportunity step: Write down a list of your passions today.

Now is the operative word.
Everything you put in your way
is a method of putting off the hour
when you could actually be doing your dream.
You don't need endless time and perfect conditions.
Do it now. Do it today.

—Barbara Sher

Obstacle 44:

Garrulity

"Stumbling with your feet is safer than stumbling with your tongue."

—Arabic Proverb

GARRULITY guarantees isolation. Talk. Talk. Talk. That's all you do. Talk. Talk. Talk. Talking too much offends people.

Garrulity is dysfunctional. Being talkative is a mask for nervousness. Settle your discomfort by listening more. Tune in to others. You can also offset garrulity by initiating conversation around current events or by asking for the opinion of others.

Live a friend-filled life, more as a listener than as a gabber. Silence is not a phobia. Don't fear stillness. Reticence is okay. You will not be overlooked if you are quiet. Instead, talk substantively so that when you do talk, people listen.

Calm your nerves. Practice silence. It is better to be listener sometimes. Show interest in other people. Pay close attention to what they are saying their needs and interests are too. Win as a communicator—one who talks and listens to others.

Be quiet.

Opportunity Step: Listen more today.

Silence is golden.

Obstacle 45:

Greed

"Fame is a vapor, popularity an accident, riches take wings and only character endures."

—Horace Greely

Greed gags giving. A selfish nature, based on greed, is not a character trait of an achiever. A selfish quest for what you can get rather than what you can give breeds myopia.

Greed diverts goal attainment. An insatiable, greedy appetite for more money or recognition distracts ones focus. And, as with any type of life imbalance, greed precipitates other obstacles. One real danger is eventual isolation. People dislike opportunistic personalities.

Selfishness or greediness is a violation of trust in a relationship. Relationships count as you build your success. Therefore, whether others can trust you or not, although subtle, is invaluable to your success. Greed hurts.

Practice giving more. Be altruistic, give more than you receive and then give some more. You will find that you actually have more than you ever had because the universe returns at least ten-fold what you selflessly give. Great people give.

Give.

Opportunity Step: Do a "Pass It On" act today.

The twin killers of success are
impatience and greed.

—Jim Rohn

Obstacle 46:

Grief

"The place from which you started at the beginning seemingly a long time ago, will now appear very close as if you had started but recently"

—Native American proverb

GRIEF grinds growth. There is no grief which time does not soften and heal. Be patient with yourself and others as you grieve. But gradually restore moments of enjoyment in your life. Sadness is the legacy of the past.

Symptomatic grief is traumatic. Not releasing your loss is like ingesting dead weight. Accept comfort. Cry and take time to mourn. Then, begin to re-embrace life. Recharge your emotional and social energy. You are still alive.

Life is to be lived! Wrenching grief should be temporary because it forces you to live in the past. Live in the present. Shift and see the right here and now. Keep memories of loved ones alive by the contributing work you do.

When you feel that you are ready, tell your story. Doing so, for the benefit of others who are grieving, is therapeutic. It relieves your mind and refreshes your spirit. Sharing is good.

Share.

Opportunity step: Volunteer in memory of a loved one today.

HAIKU

Pure sun shine down on
weeping willow souls, grieving
for lost soul and seed.

—Elizabeth Bowers
Pieces of the Tapestry

Obstacle 47:
Guilt

"Guilt is the mafia of the mind."

—Bob Mandel

GUILT gainsays growth. It is a wasted emotion. Useless guilt retards success. Instead, spend your energy on your goals. Achievement releases the past, not re-worrying the past.

Guilt stalks your mind; it is the gift that keeps on giving. In order to grow beyond guilt, learn to focus your thoughts in the present and visualize future successes. However, if you find that you need to act in order to rid yourself of guilt then do it. Do it now! Apologize, send a note, call the person or arrange to meet them for lunch or dinner. It is imperative that you deal with the issue blame-free and let it go.

Stop replaying the overviewed "what if" video. Release it. Festering guilt causes mental magnification; you tend to blow situations out of proportion when in actuality the situation may not have been that "large" after all. Don't own what is not yours.

Once you have done all you can do, get over it. Postponed guilt drains you and stalls success. Dump it. Your life is waiting!

Be happy.

Opportunity step: Buy flowers for yourself today.

Our duty is to preserve
what the past has to say for itself,
and to say for ourselves
what shall be true for the future.

—John Rustein

Obstacle 48:
Habits

"To fall into a habit is to begin to cease to be."

—Miguel de Unamuno

HABITS harm personal progress. Habits confiscate opportunity when they breed complacency. The more you rely on habit to govern your daily thinking and activity, the more you shut off learning, exploration, and the discovery of new ideas.

Some habits are beneficial; you know what and when to do specific tasks. Automatically this averts many mundane decisions. On the other hand, automatic attachment to habit can actually induce stress if new situations confound you because you are so habit-bound.

Never become constrained by habit. Read a book upside down or right to left for a few minutes, play a new game, memorize a poem, drive down a different street, explore a new store. Engage your mind differently so that you interrupt restraining habits.

Sow an act, and you reap a habit;
Sow a habit, and you reap a character;
Sow a character, and you reap a destiny.

—G. D. Boardman

Restrictive habits are made to be broken.

Opportunity step: Take a new route home today.

I am your constant companion

I am your greatest helper or heaviest burden.
I will push you onward or drag you down to failure.
I am completely at your command.
Half of the things you do you might just as well turn over to me
    and I will be able to do them quickly and correctly.
I am easily managed – you must merely be firm with me.
Show me exactly how you want something done and after a few
    lessons I will be able to do them quickly.

I am the servant of all great men; and alas, of all failures as well.
Those who are great, I have made great.
Those who are failures, I have made failures.
I am not a machine, though I work with all the precision of a
    machine plus the intelligence of a man.
You may run me for profit or run me for ruin – it makes no
    difference to me.
Take me, train me, be firm with me, and I will place the world
    at your feet.
Be easy with me and I will destroy you.

Who am I?
I am HABIT.

—John Maxwell
Thinking for a Change

Obstacle 49:

Hardship

"Fire is the test of gold; adversity of strong men."

—Senecal

HARDSHIP heralds honor. Experiencing only ease can be a handicap. Hardships are an indissoluble part of existence. Protecting yourself therefrom can be a success barrier if it causes you to over deliberate.

To survive and cope through hardship you must have fortitude; it is the backbone of the successful. You can better cope by: facing the situation realistically, focusing on solutions, realigning your goals, and/or by implementing new practices.

Hardships seem inevitable given the rate and scope of recent calamities. Rather than retreat, thinking of hardship as punishment, strengthen your resolve. In many regards, a hardship is a pre-test of success. It is often a determiner of the great. Each hardship conceals a life lesson, probe for its answers.

The extended value of hardship is that it teaches compassion. It builds determination, fortifies one's faith, and it amplifies ones character. Proverbially, hardships are a blessing in disguise.

Embrace hardship.

Opportunity step: Ask: What have I learned today?

Rene Godefroy, speaker and author of No Condition is Permanent!, knew hardship at an early age. He vividly remembers his childhood growing up in a small village in Haiti often meagerly surviving daily with only one meal. His mother left him in the care of a village lady at nine months while she went to Port-au-Prince to work, he fought disease and poverty.

He was very, very poor. To fend against hunger and poverty, Rene began to climb coconut and mango trees looking for food. He walked long distances on dangerous roads to collect drinking water and wood for cooking. His diet consisted mainly of breadfruit, which he ate so much of his belly became distended. He was always hungry.

In spite of the dire poverty he experienced, Rene had dreams. He wanted to come to America. Others, including family, laughed at him, but he persistently believed in his future in America. He came to America as a stowaway with only five dollars, two shirts and a pair of pants. He worked hard to become the American Success. He learned English, read voraciously and is now one of America's sought after, premiere motivational speakers. Back in Haiti he is the Village Hero who has established a foundation to build schools and a hospital for his village.

(Rene Godefroy, The Village Hero)
info@villagehero.com

Obstacle 50:
Hatred

"Hatred is a feeling which leads to the extinction of values."
—Joe Ortega y Gasset

HATRED hinders kindness. The infectious nature of hatred multiplies exponentially until ones existence becomes demonic. The success minded argue against hatred, they embrace lenity.

Success is joy; hatred robs joy. Investigate the basis of your truth, question assumptions, initiate conversations with those of other races, and learn the customs of other cultures.

You will be able to build empathetic relations with diverse cultures as you operate your success strategies. Honor your heritage and the heritage of others. The more you know about others, the more you grow.

Hatred is limiting. It devalues goodness. Man's first instinct is to love. Love is the pathway to success. To live with hatred—whether it's bigotry, sexism, or classism—implies an attitude of superficial superiority. Free yourself! There is so much to learn, hatred should never be the subject.

Cultivate love.

Opportunity step: Be kind to a person of another culture today.

Michael Weisser and his wife know the pain of hatred. This Nebraska family was literally stalked by Larry Trapp because they are Jewish and he was taught to hate Jews. Trapp would call their home daily leaving livid anti-Semitic messages and death threats.

One day Weisser decided to begin returning Trapp's calls. He asked him when they could meet to talk and get to know each other. After four months, Larry finally agreed. They discovered they had a lot in common. Larry eventually admitted that his false perceptions which he was taught as a member of the Ku Klux Klan were indeed wrong.

Soon after, Trapp resigned from the Klan and he publicly apologized for his unfounded hatred and mistreatment of the Weissers. He endured taunts and death threats, but he would not return to the Klan. Soon thereafter, Trapp became deathly ill and with no family who would care for him, Michael and his wife welcomed him into their home where he stayed until he died.

"To hate and to fear is to be psychologically ill. It is, in fact, the consuming illness of our time."

—H. A. Overstreet

Obstacle 51:
Ignorance

"The function of education is to teach me to think intensively
and to think critically. Intelligence plus character – that's
the goal of true education."

—Martin Luther King, Jr.

IGNORANCE ignores intelligence. It jades the attainment of success. Unintelligent, ignorant people who stagnate and refuse to learn
or adapt to progress do not succeed.

> "Ignorance never settles a question."
> -Disraeli

Ignorance is diametrically different from being uneducated.
Throughout history uneducated people have commanded armies, led
slaves to freedom, written classic prose or designed complex struc-
tures. Although uneducated by traditional norms, civilization
advanced.

A lack of education is not an excuse to stalemate your success. If
you lack certain knowledge, participate in distance learning classes,
read about new trends, begin a self study course, go to night class or
upgrade your skills in a continuing education or certificate program.
Ignorance therefore is not a virtue; it's an insipid vice that repels success. Find a mentor. Ask questions and study patterns of success.

Illuminate your mind.

Opportunity Step: Study new topics on the internet today.

Not to know is bad,
not to wish to know is worse.

—Nigerian proverb

Obstacle 52:

Impatience

"We expect more of ourselves than we have any right to."
—Oliver Wendell Holmes, Jr.

IMPATIENCE increases distance. It takes time for an oyster to make a pearl. It takes time to build a skyscraper. It takes time to actualize success.

Banish impatience if you intend to achieve your dreams. Hyrum W. Smith of Franklin Planning says "great people achieve more because they are both pragmatic and patient." Successful people plan success.

Plan your success. Develop long and short-term goals. Begin by writing a daily goal related task list. Specify each step you must take. If this is a new process for you, do not become impatient and discard your goal list as unproductive. It is not. If you are already practicing daily goal setting, add stretch goals so that you don't grow impatient. Each incremental victory is another step on your fulfillment journey. Be patient; there are no overnight successes.

Impatience clouds your vision. It obscures dreams. Success often-times, no matter much you push or propel, cannot be rushed. Dreams never ripen before their time.

Plan for your victory.

Opportunity step: Walk at a slower pace today.

When you get to the end of your rope,
tie a knot and hang on.

—Franklin D. Roosevelt

Obstacle 53:
Inertia

"Action speaks louder than fear."

—Dr. Mark Goulston

INERTIA impedes action. Staying planted in one place, no matter how comfortable you are, is a success disaster. Progress demands activity.

Advancement defeats stagnation. If you find yourself settling for less than your potential, being inert camping out in a comfort zone, ask yourself two questions:
1) What am I avoiding and why?
2) What would I do if I knew I could not fail?
Honest answers to these questions will re-energize you and restore your focus.

Act and continue to act. Combine focused concentration with active movement and an identified goal to maximize your potential for success. Combat unproductive inertia, time waits for no one.

CorpJester® Al Wiseman, of Wiseman International, says "Eat your Ps" to combat inertia. "Realize your Potential, Discover your Purpose, Stand on Principle, Live Life with Passion."

Ignite your spirit!

Opportunity step: Go out and dance today.

Miss America 1995, Heather Whitestone, choose dance as her competition talent. She danced, even though she was once stricken with a childhood illness that left her deaf and so weathered that she could not walk. Heather not only walked again, she learned how to dance.

Doctors told Heather's parents that she would never learn beyond a third grade education and that she would never again speak. But, they disbelieved this prognosis and choose to love and teach their child as if she had total capacity.

In her autobiography, Listening With My Heart, the former Miss America shares her touching story so that others will know that dreams can and do come true in spite of seemingly formidable odds. She queries, "I want you to know that dreams do come true. If they didn't why would God design our hearts with the capacity to yearn for something greater than ourselves?"

Heather now speaks louder than most, even when whispering. She not only regained her voice, she learned how to waltz in the dance of life.

Life is a dance. Enjoy the music.

Obstacle 54:
Intellect

"Knowing others is intelligence; knowing yourself is true wisdom.
Mastering others is strength, mastering yourself is true power."
—Lao-Tzu Founder of Taoism'

INTELLECT instills knowledge. To know is to know but the caveat is to realize that it is how you apply what you know that makes the difference.

It is good to study and/or have letters of advanced degrees after your name. Moreover, it is as important to be aware of your self concept. How you think about yourself and who you are is as great a benefit to your progress. When your personal concept is abrim with healthy, realistic expectations, you manifest greatness. Winners are intellectuals who know and believe in themselves.

Build your intellect and self worth daily by listening to or reading inspiring messages, studying actual patterns of other achievers, and spending your time in positive, growth environments.

Intellect is important and so is experience, common sense, and a healthy self-worth. The combination thereof sustains success.

Learn well.

Opportunity step: Spend time with an elder sage today.

If you have knowledge,
let others light their candles in it.
                              -Margaret Fuller

Obstacle 55:

Interruptions

"Few things move as quickly as the future."

—Bernard Williams

INTERRUPTIONS interfere with progress. Needless interruptions disrupt the flow of success. The direction of which is up to you. You can direct your progress.

Audit your time. Overworked people often fail. If you have voice mail and caller ID, let the service answer the call unless it is important to you or the tasks at hand. You can better manage people traffic by either scheduling appointments or establishing a time frame for "open door" type conversations. If requests from others interfere with your productivity time, the best response is "No. I can't stop what I am doing at this time. Let's schedule an appointment." This way your progress is sustained. No is a complete sentence.

The discipline required to say NO is a valuable time saver. Instead of letting others or their activities determine your daily pace and outcome, you can train others by setting your success parameters. Use time wisely. Never allow interruptions to control you, instead make sure that you deliberately establish control over them.

Say no.

Opportunity step: Turn off the television or telephone today.

I have only just a minute,
only sixty seconds in it;
forced upon me, can't refuse it.
Didn't seek it, didn't choose it.
But it's up to me to use it.

I must suffer if I loose it,
give account if I abuse it.
Just a tiny little minute,
but an eternity in it.

—Benjamin E. Mays

Obstacle 56:

Intimidation

"Keep away from people who try to belittle your ambitions.
Small people always do that, but the really great make
you feel that you, too, can become great."

—Mark Twain

INTIMIDATION infringes upon greatness. Situations and people infringe on the attainment thereof. You cannot be intimidated unless you agree. Be firm.

Don't say yes when you want to say no. Disallow intimidation. The act of intimidation is grounded in fear. It is a result of a feeling of lack of control. Restore control. Regardless of the tone or the threat, never relinquish your ambition. Combat intimidation by knowing your needs.

Resolutely know what you must do in order to succeed. Make priority lists of tasks and subtasks of each goal. Obstacles, or fear-based intimidation, happen only when you take your eyes off of your goals. Prisoners of war, political and religious captives, or those who are repressed commonly use prayer and/or vivid mental images to maintain their supremacy regardless of how intimidating the situation. Never accept intimidation.

Affirm your greatness.

Opportunity step: Say no to power drainers today.

Nien Cheng stared down intimidation. Even though her life was threatened daily in a Chinese prison and she was deprived of basic human rights, she never allowed her captors to crack her resolve.

In August 1996, Nien Cheng was arrested. Her eloquent home was invaded and ransacked. She, at age 51, was taken to the Number One detention house where she would remain, imprisoned in solitary confinement for seven years.

She was accused of being an American spy. To break her resolve, her only daughter, Meiping, was murdered. Nien Cheng never broke.

She never gave in; she dogmatically maintained her innocence. Even when her former friends pleaded with her to confess a lie, indomitable Nien chose imprisonment.

She was released in 1973 and forced to live in poverty. Although penniless, she survived even though always under watch in her Communist homeland. Nien's petitions for a visa were always denied until once she was granted an exit visa to come to the United States to visit family.

Ms. Cheng now lives in the Washington area in a peaceful, simple lifestyle. She embodies the nobility of the human spirit.

Obstacle 57:

Irrationality

"Nothing is as liberating as joy. It frees the mind and fills it with tranquility."

—Rebbe Nachman of Breslov

IRRATIONALITY ignores reality. Fundamentally the lack of rational ideals, goals or decisions is due to fear or mental disease.

Irrationality debases competence. Fear weakens ones certainty. Free yourself. Paradoxically, the other side of fear is freedom. It is curative to take one step at a time or to make one decision at a time. Practice making rational, deliberate informed choices that affect your current situation.

Boost rationality by controlling your inner thoughts. Maintain a positive, healthy outlook rather than anticipate doom. Be realistic and judiciously face each incident without fear.

Set actionable goals. Create early success. Do not set overly ambitious goals, with multi-layered stages, which become detriments to your mental attitude. Take progressive baby steps, build your confidence. Act rationally, plan well, ask for help, find a mentor, read and research, study other successful people.

Just do it.   —Nike Slogan

Opportunity step: Decide to do something different today.

What the fool cannot learn
he laughs at
thinking that by his laughter
he shows superiority
instead of latent idiocy

—Marie Corelli

Obstacle 58:

Jealousy

"All jealousy must be strangled in its birth, or time will soon make it strong enough to overcome the truth."

—Sir William Davenant

JEALOUSY jinks progress. You cannot operate successfully or achieve greatness if you are jealous of others. Invariably, you fail because your focus is misdirected.

Jealousy is insular. It is short sighted to think what you have is not enough. You have enough talent, enough possessions, and enough strength to transcend the limitation of jealousy. Tell yourself a different truth that focuses on your perfect ability to achieve.

Don't compare yourself to others. Successful goals are based on improving personal performance rather than competitive comparisons that lead to frustration. Concentrate on what is best for you.

Create a success system. Successful people do not indulge jealousy. They have greater things to do and so do you. Whatever you are jealous of is immaterial to your growth. Get over it.

You are good enough.

Opportunity step: Volunteer at a shelter today.

In jealousy there is more
of self-love than of
love to another.

—LaRochotoucauld

Obstacle 59:

Judgment

"If you judge people, you have no time to love them.".

—Mother Teresa

JUDGEMENT jaundices the soul. There are no perfect people so don't waste your time or talents judging imperfections in others. Mistakes are a common human frailty.

Exacting judgment upon yourself or others disaffirms success. Since, according to the law of cause and effect, all thoughts cause an outcome, deliberately refrain from judgment. Instead consciously practice being judgment free. Begin today by pledging to rid your mind of all forms of judgment. Affirm rather than condemn so that you manifest the effect you desire—success.

For instance, it is judgmental to fault-find. Although in many environments negativity is rampant, you can change the situation by vowing to not participate in indicting another. Surround yourself with progressive supportive people. This one act adds gigantic momentum to your success.

Don't judge yourself or anyone else for one month. For the next thirty days look for the good. You will notice a higher level of achievement. Practice compassion.

Be more empathetic.

Opportunity step: Practice unconditional acceptance today.

There is nothing noble
about being superior to some other man.
The true nobility is in
being superior to your previous self.

—Hindu proverb

Obstacle 60:
Kismet

"Choice, not chance, will determine our destiny."

—Unknown

KISMET kindles progress. It forms your destiny. The action that you take, the choices you make, the preparation you undergo and the goals you work to attain equal your kismet.

The kismet formula is simple:

$$\frac{\text{Action + Preparation}}{\text{Choice}} \times \text{Persistence} = \text{SUCCESS}$$

This success formula is universally proven. The core reason is that when you take action, prepare and persistently focus on your goals, you are acting in the sphere of self-control and discipline. Test the formula in your life.

It is human nature, to question one's destiny. The answer forms the basis of inner peace. Ask yourself: Why was I born? Mediate on your responses to discover your unique purpose as you systematical-ly process the pursuit of kismet.

Take action. Be persistent. Make informed choices. Prepare and consistently progress. Find your purpose. Experience kismet.

Choose success.

Opportunity step: Write your own success formula today.

Author James Weldon Johnson says he "had no other choice but to write." Others share the same sentiment when they are in their power. Winners often say they felt compelled as if they had no other choice but to sing, dance, play sports, design a patent, open a business or whatever is their natural proclivity.

They had no choice. It is their kismet, destiny, to be who they are. Sadly, there are millions of people who are not in their kismet zone. They don't know what they are destined to do.

It is time to figure it out or confirm that the choices you have made are a part of your true and authentic self. To assist in this self discovery, ask yourself four questions:
1. Is what I am doing contributing to my happiness?
2. Is my choice based on my natural ability?
3. Is there something else I'd rather do?
4. Is this working for me?

Once you have clarified your destiny by mentally clearing away limiting doubts and have found your true center of existence, start using the Kismet formula immediately.

Obstacle 61:

Knowledge

"To be proud of learning is the greatest ignorance."

—Anonymous

KNOWLEDGE kicks success up a notch. Information is power. A derivative of an old adage is true, Give a man a fish and he eats for a day. Give him knowledge and he opens a fish market.

Innovation is born out of a quest for knowledge. The innovator asks, why is this not so? and proceeds to devise a better way. Knowledge is a pathway to success.

On the other hand, being a know-it-all can retard creativity. Even if you are an expert in your chosen field, commit to broaden your knowledge scope by learning other new things   Experience opera, new languages, museums, books, seminars, workshops, countries, or affiliate with people who are doing what you desire to learn. Knowledge is a veritable treasure. Examine your knowledge base. Search for limiting knowledge. Weed it out; completely get rid of it and replace it with knowledge guided by a belief in unlimited potentiality. Develop a persona of wisdom for growth; that is the lodestone of success.   Be a life-long learner.

Learn and grow.

Opportunity step: Read for power today.

One day a student was asked a complicated question by his teacher. Pridelessly, the first grader rubbed his head and blurted out, "I don't know. I've only been in class 10 minutes."

(Contributed by Ms. Jacqueline Harper)
Brooks Co. Schools

Obstacle 62:

Laziness

"The great successful men of the world have used their imagination.
They think ahead and create their mental picture in all its details, fill-
ing in here, adding a little there, altering this a bit and that a bit, but
steadily building - steadily building."

—Robert Collier

LAZINESS limits options. It shortchanges your success. Many
give up too soon not realizing that it takes only a little more effort to
succeed. It may be only one more book, one more step, or one
more task before you arrive at success's threshold.

The antithesis of laziness is action. Get involved, do more. Tire
yourself out in the pursuit of your dreams. Dig in and relentlessly
take charge. It takes kinesis to grow. It takes movement to go.

Laziness is laborious. Behavioral experts say it takes more effort to
sit around and be lazy. The detriment is that your mind and body
atrophies over time if you are lazy and it takes enormous effort to
restart or recharge your dreams. Stay active and achieve.

Action works harder than idleness.

"Just give me a place to stand and I will move the world."

—Archimedes

Opportunity step: Take a fast walk today.

Pat Summit, head coach of the Tennessee Lady Vols, is named one of the best coaches—male, female, college or pro. She has set an astounding record as coach of this team since 1974, winning three NCAA championships in a row.

In Reach for the Summit Pat shares her formula for success. She calls it the "Definite Dozen System". The obstacle of laziness is not one of the dozen. Laziness is not in her vocabulary.

As a girl, growing up on a farm in Conklin, Tennessee, she learned the first lesson in her Definite Dozen System—responsibility. Her father taught her and her siblings to own what they do. Each child, irrespective of age or size, was assigned daily chores and nothing or no one superceded them. By age ten, she says, she was driving a tractor, setting tobacco, and bailing hay.

Every one of her players know Pat's Definite Dozens by heart; they are ingrained as part of the team's ethic. She uses her formula to teach, reform and discipline her players for greatness.
Former player, Chamique Holdsclaw says it is an honor to be "Summitized".

Obstacle 63:

Losing

"Success is 99% failure."
> —Soichiro Honda, Founder of Honda Motorcorp

LOSING livens living. Giving up is so easy to do. To be a winner it takes fortitude to remain determined after a loss. For many overcoming a loss often inspires a winner mentality.

Loosing can drive one to succeed. Pouting over a loss is nonsensical. Blaming others, events, or situations is the weak voice of a looser. Winners move on and move up. Jewel Diamond Taylor, in Success Gems asks "Are you in the Diamond (fast) lane" of life? Query where you would be if you experience a loosing setback. Are you on the curb, median or sidewalk waiting for an updraft to move you? Never despair.

The spirit of the winner is in you! It is in everyone. The difference is in the "inner" you. Are you afraid? Are you timid? Are you vengeful? The chief cause of winning or losing is the inner-me.

The "inner" of a winner is indomitable, courageous, and confident. Look inside yourself and examine your inner traits. If they are not winners, throw them out.

"Even if you lose, you win."   —Elie Wiesel

Get in the fast lane of life.

Opportunity step: Speed up your step today.

The Ten MOST Powerful Two Letter Words

IF
IT
IS
TO
BE
IT
IS
UP
TO
ME

Thomas B. Smith

Obstacle 64:

Luck

"I am a great believer in luck, I find the harder I work,
the luckier I get."

—Thomas Jefferson

LUCK limits ownership. Depending on the folly of luck is limiting.
Good or bad, luck is still a by-product of labor. It is axiomatic, the
harder you work, the luckier you get.

Nothing replaces effort. Even if you win the lottery, success still
requires persistence. A singer must rehearse. A painter must paint.
A pianist must practice. A speaker must speak. Whatever your talent
or goal, luck is only a small element in the process of success, if any.

Work hard. Stay focused. Believe intensely in your dream.
Recognize that only you can make your dreams come true. The
"luck" is that you worked hard for it. It has been said, that luck is
what happens when preparation meets opportunity. If you are having
"bad" luck, prepare more, work harder or re-examine the feasibility of
your goals.

Luck is a verb.

People always call it luck when you have acted more sensibly
than they have.   —Anne Tyler

Opportunity Step: Say "I am lucky" today.

Marcia Wieder in Making Your Dreams Come True, doesn't advise a dependence on luck in one's quest for success. She says that you must take active steps to fulfill your dreams.

She advocates a process of dream identification and visualization to realize a more fulsome life. In her opinion, dreams remain dreams unless you add action and planning into the pursuit.

- Get clear about what your dream is
- Remove the obstacles, especially the limiting beliefs
- Design the simple steps to make your dreams happen

Learn to face your fears, identify your limiting beliefs, and change them. To have a dream, not luck, is the first success step. You must have a dream. So, dream big! Then, plan deliberately so that your dreams come true.

Another essential step is to define your dream by vividly identifying what you want. Do this passionately. Add great detail. Know what success looks like to you. Then, write down each vivid detail, describing all elements of the dream and what you need in order to realize your dream. Visualize and vocalize your dream – crystallize it in your mind's eye.

Dreams do come true – one active vision at a time.

Obstacle 65:

Materialism

"If money is your hope for independence, you will never have it.
The only real security that a man can have in this
world is a reserve of knowledge, experience, and ability."

—Henry Ford

MATERIALISM mashes power. If your life is the pursuit of money
so that you can buy luxuries or to have more than the other guy, you
have already begun to diminish your power.

Materialism is ephemeral and its satisfaction fleeting. Keeping up
with the Jones' is futile. Rather, to give more than you get arrests
materialism. Your identity should never be wrapped up entirely in
what you have. The key to inner peace is to know your philosophy of
life and the core values that compose your identity

Ask yourself: What gives me the greatest pleasure? What elevates
my feeling of self-worth? What am I doing, or could be doing, that
engenders a sense of excellence? Honest answers to these questions underscore your ability to succeed.

You can't buy success; it is earned.

.

"It is not what you have that makes people look up to you,
it's who you are."

—Elvis Presley

Opportunity Step: Detach from luxury today.

The Prayer of Saint Francis of Assisi

Lord, make me an instrument of your peace.
Where there is hatred, let me sow love;
Where there is injury, let me sow pardon;
Where there is discord, let me sow unity;
Where there is doubt, let me sow faith;
Where there is despair, let me sow love;
Where there is darkness, let me sow light;
Where there is sadness, let me sow joy.

Lord, grant that I may seek rather to be a comfort
than to be comforted.
To understand, rather than to be understood.
To love rather than to be loved.

For it is in giving that one receives.
It is in forgiving that one is forgiven.
And it is in dying that one awakens to eternal life.

Obstacle 66:

Mediocrity

"Mediocrity is a place and it is bordered on the north by compromise, on the south by indecision, on the east by past thinking, and on the west by lack of vision."

—John Mason

MEDIOCRITY maims greatness. Settling for less than your best disguises your greatness. Remove your mask and be who you are intended to be.

Mediocrity impairs your upward reach to success. Many people often settle for less than they can achieve or for less than they deserve due to fear. In other cases they don't realize the impact of their work and therefore remain in the background. Thus, they stay beneath their greatness threshold. Ralph Waldo Emerson says, "He has not learned the lesson of life who does not everyday surmount a fear."

Surmount your fears. Let the light shine on you sometimes. There are no options to this edit if you intend to breakthrough mediocrity. Tune into your passions. Write down your goals. See the outcome you desire. Make this a part of a new daily ritual to forego obscurity. Affirm yourself everyday.

Get excited!

Opportunity step: Tell yourself I am great! today.

"The greatest cruelty in life
is not death.
The greatest tragedy is what
we let die within us."
~Norman Cousins

Obstacle 67:

Misfortunes

"Hard work spotlights the character of people: some turn up their sleeves, some turn up their noses, and some don't turn up at all."

—Sam Ewing

MISFORTUNES malign greatness. But, in the end, when you do succeed you will validate how truly great you are. Misfortune happens. It is not personal.

Misfortune is not about you; it is for you. Winners accept a misfortune and use it for wisdom. Like you, a winner, looks to discover it's purpose. Never personalize the effect of a setback. The only thing to personalize is the lesson you learn for it. Learn and move on.

Take advantage of a misfortune, work harder and smarter now because of it. Shift, but maintain your focus. For obstacles appear and are magnified the moment your focus is diverted. Keep a clear view and maintain a positive attitude. Make the necessary adjustments so that your "self" fortune expands.

Turn your stumbling blocks into stepping stones. Better yet, turn misfortune around. You might get harpo (oprah spelled backwards).

Stay focused.

Opportunity step: Ask, What am I to learn from this? today.

I want people to know my life philosophy,
to remember to play after every storm.

—Mattie Stepanek

These words spoken by 12 year old Mattie Stepanek tell the world
that he is not inhibited by misfortune. Mattie is an incredible little boy
who has a remarkable outlook on life. He was born with a rare form
of muscular dystrophy. His mom, Jeni, also has the disease and his
three siblings have already died from the disease.

Remarkably, Mattie is traveling, speaking and writing so that others
can feel his rainbow. He has appeared on The Oprah Winfrey Show,
The Today Show, and Good Morning America to awaken hearts to the
"heartstrings" of his melodious prose.

He says, "Your heartsong is your inner beauty. It's the song in your
heart that wants to help make you a better person, and to help other
people do the same. Everybody has one."

Never forget to take the time to listen to your heart.

Obstacle 68:

Misinformation

"We don't see things as they are, we see them as we are."

—Anais Nin

MISINFORMATION misuses truth. Factual information is a core element of success. You need to be well informed.

Learn all you can. Experience all you can. Become an expert in your chosen field, if you must. From time immemorial, the saying knowledge is power has proven true. Thus, it is logical that the more you know, the less likely you will be misinformed.

Take time to research questions yourself rather than rely entirely on the interpretation of others. Create your own database of facts and resources. Commit at least one hour a day learning.

Be informed; your success depends on it. The more you know, the more you will grow. Minimize mistakes. Make informed decisions. But, don't hesitate because you don't know everything. You never will. Information is fluid; it is constantly changing.

Know enough and go.

Opportunity step: Go online and study a new subject today.

Fauziya Kassindga, in her desperation to escape the ritual of genital mutilation in her native land of Togo, was misinformed about American law and was thrown into federal prison.

Bewildered and isolated, Fauziya endured the bane of prison life. There were no frills, mostly only prayer and tears. She came to America seeking a better future aware that if she returned home, she would be killed.

Her only hope was asylum in America. But, she had to convince the judge of the realness of the threat. The direness of the consequence meant that she must prevail even though she was penniless and without legal representation until attorney Layli Miller was assigned her case as part of Fauziya's pro-bono defense team.

Their work not only eventually freed Faziya, this case set multiple precedents. Immigration case law was rewritten, reclassifying female genital mutilation as a federal offense and cause for refugee immigration protection.

Sometimes, there is value in misinformation. In this case, misinformation altered justice.

The Tahirih Justice Center: http://www.tahirih.org

Obstacle 69:
Mistakes

"Experience is that marvelous thing that enables you to recognize a mistake when you make it again."

—F. P. Jones

MISTAKES magnify learning. Instead of viewing mistakes as punitive, see them as learning opportunities. Graciously accept mistakes as feedback.

Be decisive. Write down what you intend to achieve and map out deliberate steps that match your desired outcome. Concentrate on what needs to happen rather than fret over the past.

Winners are unafraid to lose, to make mistakes or fail. Achievers naturally recover by implementing a new plan or restructuring what exists. Mistakes are a part of success; they improve one's problem-solving skills. Those who avoid mistakes, avoid success.

Mistakes are commonplace. You often create more trouble when extra effort is invested in mistake avoidance. It becomes problematic, often inducing other obstacles such as indecisiveness, timidity, perfectionism, and procrastination. Elbert Hubbard says, "The greatest mistake you can make is to be continuously fearing that you'll make one." Release the fear of making a mistake. Be free.

Every mistake has a solution.

Opportunity step: Repeat: "I have learned" today.

It is common sense to take a
method and try it. If it fails,
admit it and try another.
But above all, try something.

—Franklin D. Roosevelt

Obstacle 70:
Negativity

"Flatter me, and I may not believe you.
Criticize me, and I may not like you.
Ignore me, and I may not forgive you.
Encourage me, and I may not forget you."

—William Arthur

NEGATIVITY negates optimism. It is easy to lose hope without optimism. Negative words or thoughts decimate hope. Positive thoughts inspire. You choose – optimism or despair.

Make a choice. Ask yourself, will I become consumed by forbidding thoughts or will I inspire success? Loose the weight of negativity, start a new mental exercise plan. Sit up to promise. Walk toward a dream. Stretch your capacity. Aerobicize negativity.

Examine your relationship circle too. Are the people you surround yourself with shortsighted? If so, change your environment now! Align with supportive, informed people. Clear out any negativity. Turn off your internal pessimism intercom. Let nothing and no one interfere with your primacy.

Think positive. Be optimistic. Be encouraging. Turn on the bright lights in your life. State your dreams. Begin anew; you will win.

Illuminate.

Opportunity Step: Write your life statement today.

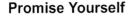

Promise Yourself

- To be so strong that nothing can disturb your peace of mind.
- To talk health, happiness and prosperity to every person you meet.
- To make all of your friends feel that there is something in them.
- To look at the sunny side of everything and make your optimism come true.
- To think only of the best, to work only for the best and to expect only the best.
- To be just as enthusiastic about the success of others as you are about your own.
- To forget the mistakes of the past and to press on to the greater achievements of the future.
- To wear a cheerful countenance at all times and to give every living creature you meet a smile.
- To give so much time to the improvement of yourself that you have no time to criticize others.
- To be too large for worry, too noble for anger, too strong for fear, and too happy to permit the presence of trouble.

The Optimist Creed
—Optimist International

Obstacle 71:

Opinionated

"The art of being wise is knowing what to overlook."

—William James

OPINIONS offset compassion. Forming opinions is a natural part of human nature. However, the character of a wise man is to sometimes maintain silence.

Because you know, or think you know, the solution doesn't allow you the privilege to state your opinion unsolicited. If there is no danger or emergency to avert, then keep quiet and allow others the chance to mature by solving it for themselves.

Ask yourself: Are my comments vital to the solution? Unless they meet this test, restrain from being the first to add your two cents worth. Save up your opinions until you have a dimes worth.

Don't be so eager to talk. You run the risk of being labeled a :"know it all". Learn when it is appropriate to say what is on your mind, but exercise restraint. Not every thing is seemly.

Solicited or not, opinions remain a personal belief until someone else adopts it. Some people do not want to be told; they want to discover their truth for themselves. Allow that.

Overlook the mundane.

Opportunity step: Practice quiet or silence today.

Watch your thoughts, they become words.
Watch your words, they become actions.
Watch your actions, they become habits.
Watch your habits, they become character.
Watch your character, it becomes your destiny.

—Frank Outlaw

Obstacle 72:

OPB (Other People's Business)

"So long as the thoughts of an individual are scattered, he will achieve no results. But, if his thinking is concentrated on a single point, wonderful will be the fruits thereof."

—Abdu'l-Baha

OPB (Other People's Business) offsets personal development. You can't work on your own growth as long as you are busy, involved in the business of another.

"Sweep around your own backyard" is an old saying that sums up appropriate counsel to a busybody. When you invest more time on the life of anyone else other than yourself, you are in denial. Many types of defense mechanisms are at work when you in OPB.

Mature into a more functional adult by minding your own business. Re-focus by going on a hike, riding in a new neighborhood, taking a class, volunteering, or writing your mission statement. The main idea is to explore what is of value to you.

The primary reason that most people fail to get what they want is due to a lack of focus. To succeed, your focus must be singular. You must isolate your goals and plan well to achieve. Make you a priority for once.

Don't be a quidnunc. Stop it!

Opportunity step: Focus on your own goals today.

Spending My Dash?

I read of a man who stood to speak at the funeral of a friend. He referred to the dates on the tombstone from beginning … to the end.

He noted that first came the date of birth and he spoke the dates with tears. But he said what mattered most was the dash between those years. For the dash represents all the time that we spend alive on this earth. And only those who loved the person know what that little line is worth. For it matters not how much we own; the cars, the house, the cash.

What matters is how we live and love and how we spend our dash. So think about this long and hard…. Are there things you'd like to change? Are there things that can still be re-arranged? For you never know how much time is left.

If we could just slow down enough to consider what's true and real. And always try to understand how other people feel. And be less quick to anger and show appreciation more. And love the people in our lives like we've never loved before.

If we treat each other with respect and more often wear a smile…. Remembering that this special dash might last a little while.

So when your eulogy is read with your life's actions to rehash… Would you be proud of the things they say about how you spent your DASH?
—Author Unknown

Obstacle 73:

Ostentatious

"Rank and riches are chains of gold, but still chains."

—Giovanni Ruffin

OSTENTACIOUSNESS odors success. Whether sweet or foul, the smell of an ostentatious lifestyle is up to you. You determine by your attitude toward riches the importance you place on them.

Riches are ephemeral. Easy come, easy go. If you can afford luxuries, by all means get and share them. But the secure, feel no need to brag or flaunt diamonds or gold. Neither determines the true final measure of your life.

If you can still be happy without rich accouterments, then you possess a healthy attitude. When riches distress your self-worth such that you feel diminished without them, you might then need to undergo a checkup.

You may need a "checkup from the neck-up" if your identity is wrapped around ostentatious riches. If a luxury car, fur, clothes, mansions or diamond rings inspire your persona, mentally detach from these material things to find the real you.

Be yourself.

Opportunity step: Spend no money today.

The ones who seek their happiness by buying
cars and clothes and rings,
don't seem to know that
empty lives are just as
empty filled with things.

—Anonymous

Obstacle 74:

Over-Activity

"Always being in a hurry does not prevent death,
neither does going slowly prevent living."

—Ibo Proverb

OVER-ACTIVITY obscures achievement. Operating with a never ending task list is to live out of balance. Winners know that balance is integral to success.

Don't allow over-activity to stretch you too thin. Minimize extraneous tasks and preoccupations. Take time to organize and plan your day. Unwind. Restore your energy and find the fulcrum that levels your balance. Walk in the park, take a vacation, relax, read with a book, or consider a new hobby. Your children and family member cherish most the things you do with them more than the things you do for them. Make quality time a priority.

Over-activity leads to stress. For some, life is so frenetic they have multi-tasked themselves to stress. Stress is a precursor to illness. Illness leads to disease. Disease leads to death. In essence, over-activity kills. Get out of the rat race.

Get into life. Stay busy, but let productivity be your motive. Better manage your time. Take it easy. Slow down and deliberate.

Enjoy life.

Opportunity step: Ask, "Why am I doing this? today.

To laugh often and much;
to win the respect of intelligent people
and affection of children;
to earn the appreciation of honest critics
and endure the betrayal of false friends;
to appreciate beauty,
to find the best in others;
to leave the world a bit better,
whether by a healthy child,
a garden patch or a redeemed social condition;
to know even one life has breathed easier
because you have lived.
This is to have succeeded.

—Ralph Waldo Emerson

Obstacle 75:
Perceptions

"What you think of me is none of my business."

—Terry Cole Whitaker

PERCEPTIONS probe reality. One pivotal life question is: "Is the glass half empty or half full?" How you perceive the waterline makes all the difference.

The most critical perception is within. How you see yourself, regardless of your public persona, determines your transcendence. It is not what others think about you that determines your makeup. It's what you think about yourself that makes the primary difference. It's not that you are indifferent to the opinion of others. It is, rather, that you are not confined by them. Live substantially by the words that you hear between your ears.

Perceptions, like first impressions, matter as long as they do not limit your true self expression. Never live afraid of what others may think or say about you. Dismiss the many "half-empty" perceptions so that in the end you leave your "half-full" indelible imprint. Make your unique mark in the world.

The future belongs to those who believe
in the reality of their dreams.

—Eleanor Roosevelt

See the real

Opportunity step: Write the real me is….. today.

Obstacle 76:

Perfectionism

"I am careful not to confuse excellence with perfection.
Excellence, I can reach for. Perfection is God's business."

—Michael J. Fox

PERFECTIONISM perpetuates stagnation. The harder you strive for perfection, the surer it is that you will be transfixed. Perfection is impossible.

You can achieve excellence. Distinguish yourself by letting "excellence" or "doing your best" be your signature. Acquire this trait by reading and remaining current in your field of endeavor. Write articles, contribute researched commentary, know your facts.

Stop waiting for the perfect moment to begin. An obsession with doing things "perfectly" is a defense mechanism that is triggered by irrationality and fear. It is erroneous to think that by waiting for perfection you eliminate mistakes or criticism. You don't. Mistakes happen and criticism is not yours to own.

Let your standards be lofty.
Let your goals be attainable.
Let your action be progressive.
Let your life be purposeful.

Leave perfection to God.

Opportunity step: Define what "excellence" means to you today.

Sir, what is the secret of your success?
a reporter asked the CEO.
"Two words."
Sir, what are they?
"Right decisions."
And how do you make right decisions?
"One word."
And, sir, what is it?
"Experience."
And, how do you get experience?
"Two words."
And, sir, what are they?
"Wrong decisions."

Obstacle 77:

Pessimism

"A pessimist sees difficulty in every opportunity, an optimist sees the opportunity in every difficulty."

—Winston Churchill

PESSIMISM permeates the soul. It breeds cynicism. Pessimism is a distorted truth which deceives so convincingly that troubles are magnified and opportunities become misshapen.

"Everything is personal, permanent, and punitive" to a pessimist, says Robin Sharma. And, what you think is often what you get. Claude Bristol in his book, The Magic of Believing, says to "know yourself" to counteract pessimism. You must "know your power…" Belief with resolute will, not pessimism, will enable you to become unconquerable" a master of men among men – yourself" he adds.

Lighten up! Laugh and have fun. Do not take yourself or your life circumstances so serious. A second from now, you will feel the difference. Believe in yourself and your abilities. You can make the impossible possible.

Neutralize pessimism by taking deliberate action. Use "I think I can" statements to command your destiny. You are in charge of your attitude and your altitude. You determine how high you go.

Don't save the laughter.

Opportunity step: Read The Little Train That Could today.

.

A small trouble is like a pebble.
Hold it too close to your eye and it fills
the whole world and puts everything out of focus.

Hold it at a proper distance
and it can be examined and properly classified.

Throw it at your feet and it can be seen in its natural setting;
just one more tiny bump
on the pathway to life.

—Celia Luce

Obstacle 78:
Piety

"Prayer indeed is good, but while calling on the Gods
a man should himself lend a hand."

—Hippocrates

PIETY proportions belief. Faith is a verb, not a noun. To believe is one thing, to have faith is another. The principal difference is that faith embodies action.

Piety is. The degree of ones piety is determined by their own thermostat. In Hebrew 11:1 faith is described as "the substance of things hoped for and the evidence of things not seen." The words substance and evidence implies performance while unseen things imply detachment.

Achievement is faith. If work is viewed as a form of worship, and if your conversations are governed by good, and your desire is to serve, then you are grounded in piety. Determine what piety feels like to you.

You can feel rich in a palace or in a bungalow. You can feel pious on a bus or in a limousine. The keystone is faith, abundant faith. To be kind, loving, caring, truthful, even daring are all applications of piety.

Ask, but detach.

Opportunity step: Ask today.

Oh, that You would bless me indeed,
and enlarge my territory,
that Your hand would be with me,
and that You would keep me from evil,
that I may not cause pain!

I Chronicles 4:9-10

Obstacle 79:
Pity

"Learning to live with your shortcomings may be the easiest way to shortchange yourself."

—Dr. Johnetta Cole

PITY poisons esteem. It is the most pervasive form of self-doubt. Seeking pity or acting pitiful means you have relinquished control. Eliminate pity, assume your power.

You are shortchanging yourself with an aimless, meandering existence when you abide pity. There is so much of life to be lived. There are so many miracles to witness. There are so many new explorations to experience.

Pity causes you to feel undeserving. To feel pity is to mistreat you. You deserve the best. Release pity. Believe in yourself. Trust.

Combat pity with:
- Affirming belief (I am somebody)
- Service to others (I am needed)
- Forgiveness (I do matter)

Acting pitiful does not serve you or this world. There is no guest list for a pity party.

Be.

Opportunity step: Affirm, serve, forgive today.

Success

You can't fell trees without some chips.
You can't achieve without some slips.

Unless you try, you'll wonder why
good fortune seems to pass you by.

Success is not for those who quail.
She gives her best to those who fail.

And then with courage twice as great
take issue once again with fate.

Tis better to risk a fall
than not to make an attempt at all.

—Unknown

Obstacle 80:

Power

"Nearly all men can withstand adversity, but if you want to test a man's character, give him power."

—Abraham Lincoln

POWER punctuates possibilities. The more power you have the more responsibility you tend to carry. The greater your power, the greater the possibility. Anything is possible when you believe you have the power to do great things.

> "Power is nothing unless you can turn it into influence"
> Condeleezza Rice.

What great things would you do if you were told that you now have the power to do them? What is your power/character trait? Would power make you different? Would you value power as a means to enrich or would you assert power abusively to manipulate or intimidate?

The answers are within you. Exercise your power; magnify its influence. Maintain a luminous character. Always know yourself, then you will not be dissuaded by power.

A strong man masters others. A truly wise man masters himself.

—Taoist proverb

Magnify your power.

Opportunity step: Help someone today.

Drinking From the Saucer

I've never made a fortune, and I'll make one now,
but it really doesn't matter 'cause I'm happy anyhow.
As I go along my journey I'm reaping better than I sowed;
I'm drinking from the saucer 'cause my cup has overflowed.

We don't have a lot of riches and sometimes the going's tough.
But while we've got our kids and friends to love us
I think we're rich enough.
I'll just thank God for the blessings that His mercy has bestowed.
I'm drinking from the saucer 'cause my cup has overflowed.

If He gives me strength and courage
when the ways grows steep and rough,
I'll not ask for other blessings, I'm already blessed enough.
May we never be too busy to help bear another's load.
Then we will all be drinking from the saucer.
All our cups will overflow.

—Unknown
(Contributed by Phillip Van Hooser)
www.vanhooser.com

Obstacle 81:
Pretentiousness

"Always keep your head up, but keep your nose at a friendly level."
—Max L. Forman

PRETENTIOUSNESS presents falsities. When the foundation of your existence is a façade, upkeep is hard. It takes money and extra-ordinary effort to maintain a panned deception. To succeed, spend time focusing on your plans and goals.

Pretension is a protective cover. It often hides fear, conceit, and the need to control issues. Thus, it takes more and more to satisfy the deepening well of these insecurities. Dr. Alan Downs calls this spiral-ing syndrome "chronic discontent". Never ever allow yourself to be manipulated by the draining instability of pretense.

Cultivate intimacy, rather than pretentiousness. Let your guard down. Be seen and known as you truly are. Be entirely honest, it is the mark of a healthy relationship. No legacy is as rich.

Get real. Don't make others work overtime going through a labyrinth of pretentious layers to get to know you. Shed the mess, build your success.

Be yourself.

Opportunity step: Ask yourself, Who is the real me? today.

Lots of people want to ride with you
in the limo, but what you want
is someone who will take the
bus with you when the
limo breaks down.

—Oprah

Obstacle 82:
Pride

"When you win, say nothing. When you lose, say less."

—Paul Brown

PRIDE promotes self. Mirror, mirror on the wall, who's the proudest of them all? Let it not always be you. Self-centered pride is vain.

Pride has its place. Be proud when you have done well, it builds esteem. But, also be proud of others' accomplishments as well, it builds compassion. Success is not always exclusively about you. Be gracious enough to acknowledge the contribution of others.

If you would rather die before you ask for help, you have too much pride. If you are overly suspicious, viewing everyone as a competitor, you have too much pride. If you find it difficult to compliment others, you have too much pride.

Don't be misdirected by the façade of pride. If you have done your best, the world will recognize it. If you assisted another, the universe will reward you. If you have shared and given what you have, the heavens rejoice with you. That is enough.

Pride is earthy.

"The ego needs recognition.
The spirit does not need to thank itself."

—Stuart Wilde

Opportunity step: Acknowledge someone else's success today.

Never let pride be your guiding principle.
Let your accomplishments speak for you.

—Morgan Freeman

Obstacle 83:

Procrastination

"The way to be nothing is to do nothing."

—Edgar Watson Howe

PROCRASTINATION prunes greatness. When everything is a rush in your life because you waited until the last minute to start, you are shortchanging yourself. Procrastination exacts a costly price.

I'm late. O my, once again, I am late. If this is a common refrain of yours, you are either settling for mediocrity or setting yourself up for failure. Either way, the outcome is an eventual calamity.

The adrenaline rush from living life on the edge is okay for a while. But to camp out in this zone implies a selfish, probably unspoken, sense that the world waits on you. What an onus deception.

To procrastinate is indefensible. Keep a calendar—quarterly, monthly, weekly or daily—you decide which schedule works best for you. Start a new habit: Schedule your time and your tasks so that you are not always in a rush, working on borrowed time.

Haste often makes waste. Don't waste your time or someone else's time rushing to and fro. Instead, act with deliberate discipline so that your achievement record is well planned.

Plan your success.

Opportunity step: Organize your tasks today.

Nothing makes a person more productive
than the last minute.

—Unknown

Obstacle 84:

Quandary

"The first step to getting the things you want out of life
is to decide what you want."

—Ben Stein

QUANDARY quickens defeat. Are you living like a contestant on Who Wants to Be a Millionaire, waiting to ask the audience what you should do? Better yet, pause and ask yourself, "What do I want to do?

Do you know where you are going to? You will find your place instinctively, once you settle the "fear" talk going on in your head. Carl Jung says "your vision will become clear when you look into your own heart." The next step is to figure out how to get to where your heart is guiding you. Afterwards all that's left is to go.

One objective starting point to end the equivocation of quandary is to do a skills inventory. Write down all of the things that you do well, the things that you enjoy, and the things others have told you that are "natural" for you.

Isolate your talents by seeing the emerging similarities. Now that you know "who you are", decide what you want and pursue it. Fiercely pursue your new found dreams. Write goal steps – that have definite dates of completion – and live in your purpose.

Decide.

Opportunity step: Do your skills inventory today.

Whenever you're called on to make up your mind,
and you are hampered by not having any,
the simplest way to solve the dilemma you'll find,
is simply by flipping a penny.

No, not so that chance shall decide the affair,
as you're passively standing there moping,
but as soon as the penny is up in the air,
you'll suddenly know what you are hoping.

—Piet Hein

Obstacle 85:
Racism

"Color is not a human or personal reality; it is a political reality."
—James Baldwin
Fire Next Time

RACISM retards realism. Prejudice of any kind is injurious. Whether it's ethnic, social, racial, or religious intolerance, its effect on society is calamitous.

Divisive racial attitudes are the cause of stereotypes, hatred, and social polarization. These external barriers can be overcome with compassion. First, if you are a member of the majority, do not indulge racist jokes or comments. If you are the minority, refuse to internalize the negativity. Be indomitable. Validate yourself. Stay focused on your success.

The pain of racism runs deep. It's manifested in the arousal of intense suspicion, fear, territorialism, and pride—all of which are self-devaluing obstacles made unnecessary because it has been scientifically proven that as a species, mankind is genetically more alike than different.

Racism is man-made. You can attack its haunting spirit by deliberately befriending someone from another ethnic group. Be kind to one person at a time, it's the human thing to do.

Embrace diversity.

Opportunity step: Talk to a person of a different race today.

"Diversity:
The art of thinking independently
together."

—Malcolm Forbes

Obstacle 86:

Regret

"Regret for the things we did can be tempered by time; it is regret for the things we did not do that is inconsolable."

—Sydney J. Harris

REGRET retrenches success. It binds the heart. No one lives perfectly, so there are always instances of regret. The valued distinction is that success minded people don't wallow in it.

Give up the past, live in the now. Musings such as: "I wish", "If only", "Back when" breed despair. It takes hope, not regret, to see the end you have designed for yourself. Forgo regret.

Backing up to the stop sign of regret is futile. You cannot turn back the hands of time. Hindsight is great, everything functions properly with it. If you need to make a "you" turn in your life, do it and move on. Do not linger in the road of regret. Focus on the future and keep your mind in the now.

The only reality is the present, that's why it is called a gift. Treasure it. Figure out how often incidents of regret have been repeated and make the needed change so that you can move on.

Outlive your "regrets".

Opportunity step: Have some fun today.

No Regrets

Follow your mind;
and when you doubt it,
insightfulness remains in your instincts.
Have no regrets.

Follow your instincts;
and in your quiet moments of aging,
feistiness remains in your heart.
Have no regrets.

Follow your heart;
and in reminiscing your pleasures,
joy remains in your soul.
Have no regrets.

Follow your soul;
and in the final enlightenment,
your light remains for all.
Have no regrets.

—Barbara Collier
Soul Stirrings

Obstacle 87:

Rejection

"Once you are really challenged, you find something within yourself. Man doesn't know what he is capable of until he is asked."
—Kofi Annan, UN Secretary General

REJECTION recoils greatness. For a winner, rejection fuels their resolve to finish triumphantly. Find what is within you.

Is it in you to achieve in spite of rejection? 95 percent of the population do not challenge themselves. But, tell somebody in that other 5 percent who feel they are destined for greatness that they are failures and they will move with deliberate focus to prove the naysayer wrong.

It is not what others value about you that is of ultimate importance, it is what you know you are capable of yourself that tips the scale of opportunity. If you believe you are oppressed, oppressed you are. Conversely, if you feel you have unlimited opportunities, then grand opportunities will manifest. The words you internalize correlate directly to your emotions which ultimately impact success. Tell yourself "I am the greatest".

Life is full of opportunities. You, unique among any other species, have the capacity to discriminate; to decide and choose what should be rejected as false or accepted as truth. Use the faculty of your mind to reject negative labels.

Create your identity.

Opportunity step: Repeat "I am the greatest" today.

In everything you do,
BE ABOVE AVERAGE.
Do and give more than is
expected. There is
no traffic jam on the
extra mile.
—Anonymous

Obstacle 88:

Resentment

"Resentment is like taking poison and waiting for it to kill the enemy."
—Nelson Mandela

RESENTMENT robs happiness. It takes your focus away from gratitude for the seen and unseen treasures that you already have. It is easy to resent when you don't have gratitude. With gratitude however, even within tests and difficulties, potentialities of beauty are latent in every living thing.

Be happy. To err is human. Sever your self and your soul from resentments. Life is too short and too sweet to harbor malice towards another. Live and forgive. "Forgiveness is giving up all hope for a better past." The past is completed with the downing of the sun; tomorrow brings a new day in which joy can be sung.

Psychologist Carl Thoresen at Stanford University conducted a six session forgiveness project. In his study, 259 adults were taught how to forgive. He found that anger, stress, headaches, ulcers were dramatically reduced. He says, "...to forgive is a valuable gift to yourself." He adds "forgiveness doesn't mean forgetting or condoning offenses or even reconciling with the offender, it means giving up the right to be angry."

Forgive.

Opportunity step: Examine your resentments today.

180

We don't get what we want,
we get what we expect.

—Dennis Waitley

Obstacle 89:

Revenge

"In taking revenge, a man is but even with his enemy; but in passing it over, he is superior."

—Sir Francis Bacon

REVENGE robs achievement. If your motivation is predicated on taking revenge, expect disappointment. Greatness will elude you until you reconcile the emotion.

Let revenge be a positive inspiration to achieve and realize what others said was impossible. But, never act maliciously out of revenge; the damage done is imposing for it attacks you first.

Release. Free yourself from the stricture of revenge. Work hard and diligently toward your dream. Plan the achievement of each of your goals. Visualize in vivid colors what success looks like to you. See yourself achieving! Success and a life well-lived is the best revenge you can ever effect.

Don't allow revenge to stall you. Let Go. Move on. The door to success opens inward, not outward. Look inward, imprint positive expectations. Give up revenge. Be a Success.

Advance.

Opportunity Step: Repeat: Never give up! four times today.

Sir Winston Churchill never invested in revenge even though he had reason to. It took him three years to get through eighth grade because he had trouble learning English. His teachers and school-mates taunted him. But, revenge was not his motivation.

Years later Oxford University invited him to deliver the commence-ment address. He arrived with his usual props. A cigar, a cane and a top hat. As Churchill approached the podium, the crowd rose in appreciative applause. With unmatched dignity, he settled the crowd and stood confident before his admirers. After removing the cigar and his top hat, he gazed at the graduates. Authority rang in Churchill's voice as he emphatically shouted, "Never give up!"

Several seconds passed before he rose to his toes and repeated: "Never give up!" His words thundered in their ears. There was a deafening silence as he reached for his hat and cigar, steadied him-self with his cane and left the platform.

His commencement address was finished.

"Never give up!"

Obstacle 90:

Sabotage

"Never think that you're not good enough yourself. A man (or woman) should never think that. People will take you very much at your own reckoning."

—Anthony Trollope

SABOTAGE self-destructs success. It kills momentum You've worked hard to earn accolades, don't sabotage your dream.

Sabotage is embedded fear. What happens is that instead of planning a celebration to mark your commencement, you do something devastating—like marry an abuser, quit, or adopt a new destructive habit—all mentally justified to you. These actions and those similar to it are indicators of self-doubt.

Challenge doubt. Ask: How will I handle success? Ask yourself this question often as you advance toward your goal. Better yet, intermittently role play success scenarios, vividly cast the scenery so that you are not shocked into a setback or sabotage when you reach your pinnacle.

Reconstruct your success. Don't victimize yourself with sabotage. It is deadly to your dreams. Be it. Do it. Feel it.

You are good enough!

Opportunity step: Ask, How will I handle success? today.

When you get in a tight place
and everything goes against you,
till it seems as though you could not
hold on a minute longer,
never give up then,
for that is just the place and time
that the tide will turn.

—Harriet Beecher Stowe

Obstacle 91:
Self (Ego)

"The willingness of one person to serve another for the profit of both is the essence of freedom and prosperity."

—Callen Hightower

SELF serves no one. Love yourself first but consider others too. An attitude of considerateness is an invaluable law of success. Remove selfishness. Care and concern for your neighbor removes selfish inclinations.

The ego, over emphasis of self, is a master deceiver. Being self-centered is false. Not everything is about and for you. Inevitably, the ego will make you believe that you don't need anyone else. How often do you say, I can do this by myself?

A self serving ego is a shibboleth. Don't let this label become your trademark. A healthy, balanced sense of self is pivotal to your success, prosperity, and freedom. Develop an attitude of service. Volunteer, participate in a team sport, find ways to give.

Sharing creates choices. Caring opens up options. Willingly assist someone else. Enrich your life.

Prosper.

Opportunity step: Volunteer. Help someone else today.

"The impossible just takes a little longer."

—Art Berg

Obstacle 92:
Self-Effacement

"Every man stamps his value on himself...
man is made great or small by his own will."

—J. C. F. von Schiller

SELF-EFFACEMENT severs optimism. Staying in the background limits your potential. Evading possibilities, because others don't see or know your talent, is self-destructive.

Exude ownership. Own your dreams and your talent. They were not given to you to hide nor to upstage another. You can and should declare your abilities. Let the world know you are gifted.

Paul A. Meyer says, "Determine what specific goals you want to achieve. Then dedicate yourself to its attainment with unswerving singleness of purpose, the trenchant zeal of a crusader."

Be a crusader for yourself. Accept praise, rather than efface yourself by rebuffing a compliment. Own your destiny; it is all up to you. If you don't "toot your own horn" sometimes, don't expect others to strike up the band either.

Do you remember an old song verse? "This little light of mine, I'm gonna let it shine." Don't shy away from your power. Liberate your talents, be known as the best.

Shine your light.

Opportunity step: Graciously accept a compliment today.

188

Our deepest fear is not that we are inadequate.
Our deepest fear is that we are powerful beyond measure.
It is our light, not our darkness, that most frightens us.
We ask ourselves, who am I to be brilliant, gorgeous,
 talented and fabulous?

Actually, who are you not to be?
You are a child of God.
Your playing small does not serve the world.
There is nothing enlightened about shrinking so that other people
won't feel insecure around you.

We are born to make manifest the glory of God within us.
It is not just in some of us, it is in everyone.
And, as we let our own light shine, we unconsciously give other peo-
ple permission to do the same.
As we are liberated from our own fear, our presence automatically lib-
erates others.

~Marianne Williamson
(popularized by Nelson Mandela)

Obstacle 93:
Setbacks

"Obstacles don't have to stop you. If you run into a wall, don't turn around and give up. Figure out how to climb it, go through it, or work around it."

—Michael Jordan

SETBACKS smite destiny. The bounty of a setback is that it forces you to examine your success patterns. If you are committed to your dream, setbacks only mean that you extract the lesson from it, re-adjust, and execute.

"Fall seven times; stand up eight", is a Japanese proverb that describes the mentality of an achiever. Fall down but get back up more times than you fell. Standing implies that you land on your feet ready to again run the race of success.

In your success journey, you may only have one setback or you may face multiple setbacks. When you do, find your center again by re-focusing on your goal. Don't disallow your success by irrationally rationalizing that it was not meant for you. If you had the dream, or goal, then it was meant especially for you.

Donnie McKirkin wrote, "...fall down, but get back up". Get back up again and again and again. Whatever the setback, don't give up.

"God gives burdens, also shoulders." —Yiddish Proverb

Get back up!

Opportunity step: Revise or reaffirm your list of goals today.

Willie Jolley, speaker, singer and author of A Setback is A Setup for A Comeback and It Only Takes A Minute to Change Your Life! believes that setbacks are designed for a comeback. He so believes this aphorism that he dares you to stand up to adversity. Stand up to your success, he says.

Struggle is embedded in success. Jolley asserts that the difference between those who succeed and those who collapse is that the successful possess a higher AQ (Adversity Quotient), which to him is a predictor along with IQ and EQ (Emotional Quotient).

Every setback is an opportunity. And, an opportunity is a terrible thing to waste. Out of adversity, opportunities exist for you to change and do something different. Look for the "alert" signals setbacks may provide. You may need to change a decision, goal, process step, habits or environment. But, change is great!

In A Setback is A Setup for A Comeback, Jolley offers teaching points. Some of his teaching points are:

1. The past is supposed to be a place of reference, not a place of residence.
2. See it as a setback with a comma, rather than a setback with a period.
3. Do not settle for unknown hells when you can have unknown heavens.

A setback is a set-up for a comeback; comeback even stronger.

Obstacle 94:
Sexism

"Hope is the companion of power, and mother of success; for who so hopes strongly has within him the gift of miracles."

—Samuel Smiles

SEXISM shifts power. Any unjust bias is oppressive. As with any "ism" - sexism or racism - the counterpoise is hope.

Have hope. Regardless of the societal oppression, maintain the highest level of hope and faith so that you assuredly know who you are. Find creative ways to tilt the scale of equality in order to have a more meaningful existence. Link up with others for strength; start a micro-enterprise. In cultures where women or religious minorities are proscribed, usually because of tradition or dogma, there exists a power-based sub-culture. The impact that a small group of people can effect is miraculous. Sexism devalues; belief empowers.

Establish a base of support. Empirical studies identify the value of mentoring groups and social or spiritual affiliations as chief to success and sustained achievement. Know yourself; maintain a healthy sense of identity that is inviolable. This, in itself, is a measure of success.

Empower yourself.

Opportunity step: Repeat: "I believe in me" today.

There are no circumstances around you more powerful
than the power within you.
You are responsible for your life through your consciousness.
Racism, sexism, homophobia, ageism have no power over you
unless you believe they do.
A belief is the most contagious influence you possess.
If you believe in circumstances, they can and will defeat you.
If you believe in yourself, you are assured victory.

There is a wonderful inner world at work within each of us.
It knows no color, gender or age.
We fuel this inner world with initiative, ingenuity and
a picture within our minds.

The world responds and produces according to how we fuel it.
If we picture poverty, oppression, failure, disease and doubt,
we cannot expect to enjoy wealth, success and health.
When we put the forces of our inner self to work with good thoughts,
it will keep our inner world clean, fertilize our minds with productive
positivity, the powers within will create, with dynamic force, all that we
believe is possible.

—Dr. Johnnie Coleman

Obstacle 95:

Stagnation

"Persistence is the measure of your belief in yourself."

—Brian Tracy

STAGNATION stalls success. The escapism of stagnation yields no results. Do nothing, get nothing, Work much, get much.

This syllogistic idiom sums up a cardinal rule of success. What you do and believe influences what you get. Standing still, expecting a miracle, is a definition of success insanity. Stagnation, while expecting success, is tantamount to planting a crop but not watering or fertilizing it, yet waiting for a harvest. You have to plant seeds, clean out weeds, fertilize and till the soil before a harvest is produced.

The same is true if you expect to achieve success. You have to plant expectation, clean out doubt, fertilize the dream, and till the soul before you achieve. Success requires work.

Move. Take action. Start. Do something now! The race does not belong to the slow. It is ruled by those who get up and go. Stagnate not. Don't let your dreams die and rot.

Get excited!

Opportunity step: Enjoy a fresh tossed salad today.

Commonalities of the Successful
Traits/Dimensions of Winning

1. Vision. Winners have a clear picture of what they want.

2. Action Plan. Winners have a defined strategy and committed action plan.

3. Take Action. Winners work and rally others to adopt a known outcome.

4. Take Risks. Winners take risks, not in a reckless fashion, but in a decisive, informed manner.

5. Truth. Winner deal with the facts and value honesty. They don't rely entirely on the opinion of others.

6. Nucleus. Winners have a nucleus of support.

7. Passion. Every winner has passion.

He who has a why to live for can bear almost any how.
—Friederich Nietzsche

Obstacle 96:

Stress

"Life is not a stress rehearsal"

—Loretta La Roche

STRESS suspends success. Your dreams are often placed on hold when you are tired and frazzled due to stress. Instead, pick up your dream, re-work your life patterns.

Many live at such a frenetic pace that they seldom rest enough to even daydream. Refresh yourself. Dream. Steal away for a moment. Take time. Refresh your body and soul. Meditate, or add tai chi or yoga to your relaxation regimen.

Laugh more. Divert stress. Bodily disease, mental incapacitation, depression and suicides are all rooted in stress. Relax, de-stress the distress. Not everything is an emergency.

"There is more to life than increasing its speed."

—Gandhi

You are too blessed to be stressed. Restore yourself. Go to a spa, read a book, walk on the beach, turn off the cell phone. Rest. Flex your fingers and toes.

Chill.

Opportunity step: Breathe deep. Slow down today.

5 Ways to Live Stress Free

1. Relax. Take at least five minutes in the morning to relax your body. Let your arms swing. Go limp and relax. Repeat anytime stress encroaches.
2. Laugh. Find the funny even in the absurd. Listen to or read jokes, comics, funny short stories, or watch sitcoms. Laughter is music from the soul.
3. Stop. Don't just slow down, stop. Regain your perspective. Re-assume control. Be still. Meditate. Pray. Center yourself by restoring peace.
4. Listen. Play your favorite music, listen to the birds chirping or hear children's laughter. Tune in to moods other than anxiety.
5. Breathe. Take long, slow, deep breaths. Oxygenate your cells by breathing air into your diaphragm. Increase your energy, breathe.

Obstacle 97:
Success

"Everyone is trying to accomplish something big,
not realizing that life is made up of little things."

—Frank A. Clark

SUCCESS supercedes distress. Success is stronger than failure. Regardless of how intense the failure, the spirit of victory triumphs in the mind of a winner.

"No matter how hard you try you can't stop me now" is a vamp in an old Temptations song. It signifies that success is inevitable when you develop and sustain successful habits.

Success is a habit. It's a habit that must be worked continually. Even when you have achieved one plateau, do not rest on its laurels. Instead, find more to do or other angles in the puzzle. Success, like learning, is life long. Climb higher now. You have proven that you can reach a summit. Seek other challenges, discover other solutions. Ask yourself: What new can I contribute today?

Find that new path. Explore new territories. Examine new opportunities; there is no time or talent to waste. Renew your quest for success.

Churchill says, "Success is never final". But it is sustainable.

Charge to new heights!

Opportunity step: Walk a labyrinth today.

Six Essential Qualities
that are KEY to SUCCESS

1. Sincerity
2. Personal Integrity
3. Humility
4. Courtesy
5. Wisdom
6. Charity

—Dr. William C. Menninger

Obstacle 98:
Temerity

"I am not afraid of storms, for I am learning to sail my ship."
—Louisa May Alcott

TEMERITY tames success. Being reckless, rash, or foolhardy (the definition of temerity) is irrational. These traits ensure failure. Unless tempered with focused discipline, defeat is an inevitable consequence.

Forge through failure and defeat. Learn from teachable mistakes but vow not to repeat the past. It is done for. You've got success to make. Success is not boring, build excitement into every victory. Waste not the moment or the time, due diligence is fine.

Suspend rashness. Plan well. Sail your ship on chartered waters. But by all means, go and set sail. Move out into the stream of life. Operate beyond the ordinary, but observe the rules.

Create a success system. Be not foolish. Never be anyone's fool. Use your intelligence wisely for gain. Abide by the Golden Rule.

Banish recklessness. Take control. Grab life by the horn. Go forward with confidence. Weather the storm. Only courage is spoken here.

Have fortitude.

Opportunity step: Plan all of your activities today.

Veteran racecar driver Mario Andretti may appear to have an over abundance of temerity, but he is a very pragmatic man. The sport of racecar driving is dangerous, filled with testosterone and high adrenaline. One mistake can be deadly.

For him, the recognition that death is a consequence of foolish, rash or reckless behavior drove Andretti to check and cross-check every activity in the pit and on the course. He was one of the most exciting race car drivers of all time. He won four (4) National Indy Championships, logged more than 100 victories and captured more pole positions than any other driver.

Andretti was successful not because he is foolhardy; he was successful because he studied and planned well. He says, "Desire is the key to motivation, but it's the determination and commitment to an unrelenting pursuit of your goal – a commitment to excellence – that will enable you to attain the success you seek."

He survived numerous crashes, escaped burning cars and yet took many victory laps. He used skill, not reckless temerity.

Winning is not a sport for the foolish.

Obstacle 99:
Tradition

"Emancipate yourself from metal slavery. None but ourselves can free our minds. Be rid of tradition."

—Bob Marley

TRADITION tempers originality. Maintaining tradition has its place. Learning from the past has its value. Even so, some traditions need to be abandoned for the sake of progress. You have to move on.

Maintaining the status-quo, tradition, can be a devious form of escapism. If tradition evokes stagnant complacency, it is time to jump-start your thinking. From the perspective of what is, begin to think about the "what if?".

Confront tradition. Break through stale boundaries. Challenge the norm so that your imagination inspires new successes. "Live out of your imagination, not your history" says Stephen Covey.

See new things. Question, so that you can grow. Ask why? or why not? Break the restriction of tradition. Normalcy is often boring. Have confidence to do something you have not done before. Have courage.

Test your ability to fly solo.

Opportunity step: Ask more questions today.

Success is
knowing that one human being
has breathed a little easier because you lived.
--Dennis Kimbro

Obstacle 100:
Trauma

"The gem cannot be polished without friction, nor man perfected without trials."

—Chinese Proverb

TRAUMA tramples hope. Although going through a trauma can be devastating, it is not a defeat. An unexpected event can traumatize even the most stoic. But, a winner moves on.

Disasters may cause you to be so emotionally stunned that you feel paralyzed and numb for a while. Cope with hope. Whether your trauma arises after the death of a loved one, from a catastrophe, accident, or other type of calamity, remain hopeful. A newer, brighter, and better day is only 24 hours away.

Don't turn trauma into a drama. Trauma, even though devastating, tends to clarify unanswered questions. Calamities oftentimes causes one to re-align priorities or magnify a sense of purpose.

See the world as new. Dream again even though things are different now; you've passed a test or two. Spend time with loved ones, show them that you care. Hold hands with a friend, assured there is something there. Accept the trauma for the best. Never give up. You can never lose success.

Give thanks.

Opportunity step: Donate blood, if you can, today.

"Sometimes I feel invincible" is what Monica Iken is often heard to say. She is the widow of Michael Iken, a bond broker who perished at Ground Zero, on September 11th.

Her victim-less attitude inspires audiences and mobilizes change. Her message is clear, whether to the children that she teaches in the Bronx or to the stranger in the audience. Have courage, she says. It was just that attitude, held so deeply by Mrs. Iken and thousands more, that created a movement.

After hearing about a rush to accept bids to reconstruct the World Trade Center towers or a similar structure, Mrs. Iken led the fight to delay construction at Ground Zero until a plan that included a befitting memorial honoring the nearly 3,000 victims was in place.

Although still grieving about the tragedy, Monica Iken has a voice, symbolizing that life has to go on.

> Act as if what you do makes a difference. It does.
> —William James

Obstacle 101:

Worry

"Worrying is like a rocking chair; it gives you something to do, but it doesn't get you anywhere."

—Unknown

WORRY wrecks optimism. It is the dark spot where negatives are developed. Optimism and worry cannot co-exist. You must decide which emotional end of the spectrum boosts your success. Do you subtract from (worry) or add to (optimism) your life?

Worry or optimism: It takes the same amount of energy. Actually, worry expends more energy. Worry is a withdrawal from your emotional bank account that is similar to the penalties for early withdrawal from an IRA. Worrying has the tendency to keep one preoccupied with the mundane things of life. Worry less, focus on success.

Worry is interest paid on trouble before it falls due.
—William Ralph Inge

Optimism is a deposit in your life bank account. It carries no penalty. Instead, it adds a lot of interest to your life.
Be the best in life. Live Passionately.

Be happy. Don't worry.

Opportunity step: Whistle a lot today.

Don't Ever

Don't ever be reluctant to show your feelings
when you are happy, give in to it...
When you are not, live with it.

Don't ever be afraid to try to make things better
you might be surprised at the results.

Don't ever take the weight of the world on your shoulders.

Don't ever feel threatened by the future.
Take life one day at a time.

Don't ever feel guilty about the past. What's done is done.
Learn from any mistakes you might have made.

Don't ever feel that you are alone.
There is always somebody there for you to reach out to.

Don't ever forget that you can achieve so many
of the things you can imagine.
It is not as hard as it seems.

Don't ever stop loving.
Don't ever stop believing.
Don't ever stop dreaming your dreams.

—Unknown

Book Orders

Order Information:
This book may be purchased

Websites:

www.climbeveryobstacle.com
www.wordsmithrevisions.com
www.realword.com
www.sherrellpublishinggroup.com
www.amazon.com

Mail Order Form:
P.O. Box 931461
Norcross, GA. 30093-1461

Order Form: Send Checks or Money Orders to Wordsmith Revisions

Name _____

Send to _____

Address _____

City _____ State _____ Zip _____

I appreciate you. Thank you for your support.

Websites

www.fallingawake.com	(goal setting, life planning)
www.nsaspeaker.com	(professional speaking business)
www.toastmasters.org	(public speaking)
www.selfimprovement.com	(personal development)
www.beliefnet.com	(quotes, spiritual awareness)
www.dreamcoach.com	(life fulfillment)
www.oprah.com	(women's issues, empowerment)
www.freecreditreport.com	(finances)
www.selfgrowth.com	(transformation, change)
www.lifetime.com	(life, body, mind growth)
www.nase.org	(National Association Self Esteem)
www.aboutquotes.com	(motivational quotes)
www.lifetime.com	(well-being)
www.motivationalmecca.com	(motivational quotes)
www.coachu.com	(coaching, training)
www.wordsmithrevisions.com	(my website)

Bibliography

7 Habits of Highly Effective People, Stephen R. Covey, Fireside Books, 1989

A is for Attitude, Patricia Russell-McCloud, Quill, 1999

Acts of Faith: Daily Meditations for People of Color, Iyanla Vanzant, Fireside Books, 1993

An Attitude of Gratitude, Keith Harrell, Hay House Publication, 2003

Celebrating Life, Luci Swindoll, Navpress, 1989

Choosing Happiness: The Art of Living Unconditionally, Veronica Ray, Hazleden Books, 1990

Created Rich, Patrick Barker, Naturepath Publishers, 1995

Do It! Let's Get Off Our Buts, Peter McWilliams, Prelude Press, 1991

Do They Hear You When You Cry, Faziya Kassindja and Layli Miller Bashir, Delacorte Books, 1998

Embracing Life: Growing Through Love & Loss, Dorothy Corkille Briggs, Doubleday, 1985

Embracing Uncertainty, Susan Jeffers, St. Martin Press, 2003

Esteemable Acts, Francine Ward, Broadway Books, 2003

Finding Your Own Star, Martha Beck, 3 River Press, 2001

Fortitude: True Stories of True Grit, Malinda Teel, Red Rock Press, 2000

Get Out of Your Own Way, Mark Goulston and P. Goldberg, Pedigree, 1996

Getting Unstuck, Joyce Browne, Hay Press, 2002

Gifted Hands, Dr. Ben Carson, Zondervan Publishing, 1995

God's Psychiatry, Charles L. Allen, Jove Books, 1953

Happiness Is a Choice, Frank Minirith and Paul D. Meier, Baker Book, 1978

Higher Than Hope, Fatima Meer, Harper and Row, 1988

If It Is To Be It Is Up To Me, Thomas B. Smith, Northwest, 1995

It Only Takes A Minute to Change Your Life. Willie Jolley, St. Martins, 1997

It's Easier to Succeed Than to Fail, Truett Cathy, Oliver Nelson, 1989

Keep Your Brain Alive: 83 Neurobic Exercises, Lawrence C. Katz and Manning Rubin, Workman Publishing, 1999

Let It Go, Joanna Horn, Red Wheel, 2003

Life and Death in Shanghai, Nien Cheng, Grove Press, 1986

Life is Not a Stress Rehearsal, Loretta LaRoche, 2000

Life is too Short to Wear Tight Shoes, Barbara Faison, In Search of, 2000

Life Without Limits, Lucinda Bassette, Quill, 2001

Live Your Dreams, Les Brown, Morrow, 1992

Love and Power in a World Without Limits, Terry C. Whittaker, Harper, 1990

Making Your Dreams Come True, Marcia Wieder, Harmony Books, 1999

Managing With the Wisdom of Love, Dorothy Marcic, Josey-Bass, 1997

No Condition is Permanent, Rene Godefroy, Inquest Publishing, 2002

Organize Yourself, Ronni Eisenberg and Kate Kelly, Wiley and Sons, 1997

Prescriptions for Happiness, Ken Keyes, Jr., Living Love Publications

Real Magic, Dr. Wayne D. Dyer, Harper Collins, 1992

Real Moments, Barbara D. Angelis, PhD, Delacorte Press, 1994

Reclaiming Your Power, Creativity, Brilliance and Dreams, Riverhead, 1988

Sacred Surprises: When God Turns Your Life Upside Down, Dale Hanson Bourke, Word Publishing, 1991

Say Yes to Change, George and Sedena Cleppanelli, Walking Stick, 2001

See You At The Top, Zig Zigglar, Pelcian Publications, Inc. 1989

Self-Made In America, John McCormack, Addison Wesley, 1994

Self Matter: Creating Your Life From the Inside Out, Phillip C. McGraw, Simon & Schuster, 2001

Simple Abundance: A Daybook of Comfort and Joy, Sarah Bon Breathnach, Warner, 1995

Snapshots of a Lifetime, Barbara Collier, Taylor-Made, 2000

Soul Stirrings, Barbara Collier, 2002

Spiritual Sayings of Kahlil Gibran, Anthony R. Ferris, Bantam Books, 1962

Stand Up for Your Life, Cheryl Richardson, The Free Press, 2002

Steve Jobs: The Journey Is the Reward, Young, Jeffrey S., Lynx Books, 1988

Substance and Spirit, Kysa Daniels, Clarion Communications, 2002

Success Gems, Jewel Diamond Taylor, QuietTime, 1999

Success Handbook- The Original, Joey Reiman, Longstreet Press, 1992

Success Runs In Our Race, George C. Fraser, William Morrow 1994

The Argument Culture: Moving from Debate to Dialogue, Deborah Tannen, Random House, 1998

The Art of Real Happiness, Norman Vincent Peale, D.D. and Smiley Blanton, M.D., Prentice Hall, 1950

The Be-Happy Attitudes: Eight Positive Attitudes That Can Change

Your Life, Dr. Robert Schuller, Word Books, 1985

The Courage to Create, Rollo May, Bantam Books, 1978

The Celestine Prophecy, James Redfield, Warner Books, 1993

The Dance of Anger, Harriet Goldhor Lerner, PhD, Harper and Row, 1985

The Four Agreements, Don Miguel Ruiz, Amber-Allen Publishing, 1997

The Greatest Salesman in the World, Og Mandino, Bantam Books, 1988

The Half Empty Heart: A Supportive Guide to Breaking Free From Chronic Discontent, Allen Downs, PhD, Firside Books, 2002,

The Magic of Believing, Claude M. Bristol, Pocket Books, 1948

The Magic of Conflict, Thomas F. Crum, Simon and Schuster, 1987

The Miracle of Mind Dynamics, Joseph Murphy, Reward Books, 1964

The Magic of Self Image Psychology, Maxwell Maltz, Prentice-Hall, 1964

The Noonday Demon: An Atlas of Depression, Andrew Solomon, Scribner, 2001

The One Minute Millionaire, Mark Victor Hansen and Robert G. Allen, Harmony Books, 2002

The Path to Love, Deepak Chopra, M.D., Three Rivers Press, 1997

The Power of Full Engagement, Jim Loehr and Tony Schwartz, Free Press, 2003

The Power of Now: A Guide to Spiritual Enlightenment, Eckhart Toole, New World Library, 1999

The Prayer of Jabez, Bruce Wilkinson, Multnomah Publishers, 2000

The Seven Spiritual Laws of Success, Deepak Chopra, Amber-Allen Publishing, 1994

The Winner Within, Pat Riley, Putnam, 1993

Think and Grow Rich, Dennis Kimbro and Napolean Hill, Fawcett, 1992

What Do I Want to Do With My Life, Po Bronson, Random House, 2001

What Makes the Great Great, Dennis Kimbro, Doubleday, 1998

What You Think of Me is None of My Business, Terry Cole-Whittaker, Jove Books, 1979

When I Relax I Feel Guilty, Tim Hansel, David C. Cook Publishing, 1979

Who Moved My Cheese?, Spencer Johnson, MD, G. Putnam & Sons, 1999

Why People Don't Heal and How They Can, Caroline Myss, Ph.D., Harmony Books, 1997

Why Struggle? Life is Too Short to Wear Tight Shoes, Barbara Faison, In Search of Publications, 1999

Wisdom from the Ancients: Proverbs, Maxims and Quotations. Menahem Mansour, Maryland Printing Company, 1994

Write It Down Make It Happen, Henriette Anne Klauser, Scribner, 2000

You Are the Message, Roger Ailes with John Kraushar, Doubleday, 1988

"Change is not effortless."
Thomas B. Smith

Notes Page

"You are the arbiter of your destiny. Your success is dependent upon what you accomplish in life and is measured by the degree of your self-satisfaction."   Patrick Barker